ArtScroll Series®

Rabbi Nosson Scherman / Rabbi Meir Zlotowitz

General Editors

YES YOU

Published by

Mesorah Publications, ltd

CAN!

A GUIDE TO SUCCESS IN LIFE

ARON FRIEDMAN

Translated from the Hebrew *Gam Attah Yachol* by

Esther van Handel

FIRST EDITION
First Impression ... June 2003

Published and Distributed by
MESORAH PUBLICATIONS, LTD.
4401 Second Avenue / Brooklyn, N.Y 11232

Distributed in Europe by
LEHMANNS
Unit E, Viking Industrial Park
Rolling Mill Road
Jarrow, Tyne & Wear, NE32 3DP
England

Distributed in Israel by
SIFRIATI / A. GITLER
6 Hayarkon Street
Bnei Brak 51127

Distributed in Australia and New Zealand by
GOLDS WORLD OF JUDAICA
3-13 William Street
Balaclava, Melbourne 3183
Victoria, Australia

Distributed in South Africa by
KOLLEL BOOKSHOP
Shop 8A Norwood Hypermarket
Norwood 2196, Johannesburg, South Africa

Typography by CompuScribe at ArtScroll Studios, Ltd.

Printed in the United States of America by Noble Book Press Corp.
Bound by Sefercraft, Quality Bookbinders, Ltd., Brooklyn N.Y. 11232

Preface

I n the course of years of counseling, I have seen many people who have become bogged down in life start moving forward again once they adopted a new approach.

The book began to take shape as I presented my approach to the public in lectures and in a weekly column in *HaMachaneh HaCharedi*. The reactions of thousands of readers and listeners and the comments of hundreds of people whom I have counseled honed the ideas.

Whenever Torah opinion was needed, I consulted *gedolim* and experienced educators and counselors. My thanks to all.

With awe, I offer my gratitude to the BELZER REBBE shlita for his continuous encouragement. Ever since I entered the Belzer Yeshivah in Jerusalem as a youth of 15, I have benefited from his advice in many areas. With fatherly devotion, he has taken of his precious time to enlighten me. I learned much from his deep wisdom and holy ways during the eleven years that I was privileged to serve as his personal secretary. It is the Rebbe who first guided me in learning to understand man's soul and then guided me in my work with people. From the depths of my heart I pray, "May You add days to the days of the king, may his years be like all generations" (Tehillim 61:7).

❖   ❖   ❖

I thank my father, RABBI YEHOSHUA BEN YONAH of Muzoi, Czechoslovakia, for imbuing in me a passion for truth and for the wisdom of life. A great and pious Torah scholar with sharp discernment, he earned an honest living and kept fixed times for Torah study. He had a special rapport with people, who would gather around him to drink in his words. His golden character shone in full glory during his prolonged illness, when he accepted G-d's judgment with love and did everything in his power to lighten the burden of his caregivers. He met death fearlessly on Shabbos Va'eira, 27 Teves 5741, at the age of 68.

My mother, may she live and be well, is a modest and righteous woman who instilled in her children's hearts the love of Torah and fear of Hashem. May Hashem bless her and her husband, RABBI MOSHE ZILBERMAN, a G-d-fearing Torah scholar, with many years of good health and much nachas from all their descendants.

It is my wife, NECHAMAH BEILA, who gives me the courage to help others; I could never have done it without her support. May Hashem grant her a long and happy life, and may we raise our children together in good health — to Torah, marriage, and good deeds.

Many thanks to my in-laws of blessed memory. My father-in-law, RABBI DAVID EISENBERG, was a supporting pillar of the religious community of Sao Paulo, Brazil. He kept fixed times for Torah study, worked hard to support his family, and willingly donated of his earnings to charity and Torah institutions. He was known for his hospitality; when fundraisers for worthy causes came to Sao Paulo, he hosted them and even accompanied them to potential donors. He died on 19 Nissan 5754.

My mother-in-law, MRS. MALKAH EISENBERG, was a model of modesty and good character who devoted herself to raising her children. With simple, wholehearted faith, she meticulously kept every detail of Jewish custom. She died on 17 Nissan 5746, at the age of 57. May my in-laws pray on high for all their descendants.

Thank you to MRS. ESTHER VAN HANDEL for adapting this book for the English-speaking public.

יחיאל מ. יעקבסון
ת.ד. 18
זכרון-יעקב 30900

To my dear friend, the outstanding Torah scholar, Rabbi Aaron Friedman *shlita*:

I read and reread the book that you sent me, carefully and with pleasure. The basic principles of coping that you deal with are important for every teacher and for every parent. I very much hope that these principles will become known to all, because great benefit can be gained from them. I hope that teachers and educators will study and review them. This book is required reading; our times demand it.

בברכת ידידות
והערכה עמוקה

Approbation to the original Hebrew edition

Rabbi Yechiel Yaakovson, noted Israeli educator and lecturer, founded and heads "Shema Beni" — an organization for helping at-risk teenagers.

ימיאל מ. יעקבסון
ת.ד. 18
זכרון-יעקב 30900

בעזרת החונן לאדם דעת.

כבוד ידידי היקר
התורני המופלג
הר"ר אהרון פרידמן שליט"א,
רוב ברכה ושלו!

קראתי היטב את פרקי הספר "גם אתה יכול" שהעברת אלי. קראתים פעם ועוד פעם,
בעיון רב וגם בהנאה. כי למרות שיסודות ההתמודדות הבסיסיים שבהם אתה עוסק,
חשובים הם **לכל** מחנך **ולכל** הורה, אבל עד עתה לא היתה דרך להנחילם לכלל . זאת,
משום שהחומר הקיים מנוסח בשפה כזו, שמקשה מאוד (על מי שאינו מצוי בתחום זה)
להבין את הדברים ולהפיק מהם תועלת, ומשום שחומר זה מורכב ברובו משילוב
מסוכן של תבן ובר, שקשה מאוד להפריד ביניהם.

ברור, אפוא, מדוע נהניתי מאוד לקרוא דבריך – הן מצד התוכן והן מצד הצורה.

מצד התוכן – הצלחת בס"ד לברור היטב את התבן מן הבר כך, שהחומר הזה משובח
הוא לא רק מחמת מה שכתבת אלא גם מחמת מה שלא כתבת, ולא רק דבריך
המפורשים חשובים הם מאוד, אלא שיש ערך רב גם למה שהבלעת בין השיטין של
דבריך.

ומצד הצורה – עלה בידך, בס"ד, לנסח הדברים בשפה ברורה ופשוטה, השווה לכל נפש.

מאוד מקווה אני, שדבריך יהיו לנחלת-הכלל, כי התועלת שניתן להפיק מהם – רבה
היא עד מאוד. אבל במיוחד מקווה אני, שהעוסקים בחינוך ילמדו אותם שוב ושוב. כי
לגבי מי שרוצה להימנות בין מצדיקי הרבים ־ כמדומני שהחומר הזה הוא (כיום)
בבחינת ספר חובה שעליהם לדעתו על בוריו.

אכן "דבר בעיתו – מה טוב".

בברכת ידידות
(והערכה עמוקה

בעזרת החונן לאדם דעת.

Approbation to the original Hebrew edition

EZER MIZION

Aid & Support for the Sick and Needy

National Headquarters:
16 Eshel Avraham, Bnei Brak, Israel
Tel. 03-5742742, Fax. 03-5744030
E-mail: ezer_m@netvision.net.il

עזר מציון

מרכז עזר לחולה ולנזקק
רח' אשל אברהם 16, בני ברק
מיקוד: 51561, ת.ד. 2709
טל. 03-5742742, פקס. 03-5744030

Shvat 5759

To my friend, the distinguished educator, Rabbi Aaron
Friedman *shlita,*

I am delighted to extend my blessings upon the publica-
tion of your book — the product of your rich experience in
lending an attentive ear and a warm, understanding heart to
religious Jews who need counseling.

Out of appreciation for your successful work with Ezer
Mizion in the course of several years, I can testify that that
your sources come from pure Judaism.

I am sure that all those who wish to make the most and
best of themselves, and to live happy, fulfilling lives, will
benefit greatly from your book. May Hashem give you
fresh strength to continue lighting your way so that you
can help people in distress and publish more books to
benefit the public.

בברכת חזק ואמץ,

Approbation to the original Hebrew edition

EZER MIZION

Aid & Support for the Sick and Needy

National Headquarters:
16 Eshel Avraham, Bnei Brak, Israel
Tel. 03-5742742, Fax. 03-5744030
E-mail: ezer_m@netvision.net.il

עזר מציון

מרכז עזר לחולה ולנזקק
רח' אשל אברהם 16, בני ברק
מיקוד: 51561, ת.ד. 2709
טל. 03-5742742, 03-5744030. פקס

בס"ד

חודש שבט תשנ"ט לפ"ק

לידידי ורעי המחנך הדגול
הרה"ח ר' אהרן פרידמן שליט"א

השלום והברכה.

בשמחה ובגילה הנני מצרף לך את ברכותי לרגל הופעת ספרך "גם אתה יכול", אשר בו בא לידי ביטוי נסיונך העשיר בהטיית אחן קשבת ולב חם ומבין במתן הדרכה עתירת עצה ותושיה לרבים מאנשי שלומנו, שנקלעו לבעיות שונות ומגוונות.

מתוך הערכה לעבודתך הברוכה במסגרת ארגון "עזר מציון", זה שנים אחדות, אני יכול להעיד שמעייניך נובע ממקורות היהדות הצרופה, ויותר מאלף עדים ניצבים סיפורי הצלחתך, בסייעתא דשמיא, וכל אלו מרעיפים עליך את ברכותיהם.

בטוחני שכל אלה שחשקה נפשם להפיק מעצמם את המירב והמיטב, ולחיות חיים מאושרים מלאי סיפוק, יפיקו תעלת רבה מספרך. כה יתן לך ה' כוחות רעננים להמשיך ולהאיר הדרך להיות שליח נאמן בסיוע למצוקות הכלל והפרט, ולפרסם עוד ספרים לתועלת הרבים.

בברכת חזק ואמץ,

חנניה צ'ולק
יו"ר העמותה

Approbation to the original Hebrew edition

Table of Contents

Introduction

Taking Control of Your Life

thank G-d for His unbelievable kindness in helping me throughout my life, and I pray for His continued assistance. In particular, I am grateful for receiving Hashem's help in my work of restoring people's hope and getting them back on their feet. Succeeding in my work gives me sublime joy.

It is said that words that come from the heart enter the heart. I pray that — even if you don't agree with everything I say — my words will be of benefit to you and help you to succeed in your ambitions.

To preserve confidentiality, names and descriptions of people whom I have counseled have been changed.

You Are a Winner

f you believe that the world is divided into two groups — winners and losers — you are sorely mistaken.

It is true that the world is divided into two. But the distinction is between those who know that everyone can succeed and those who do not know. From my experience in working with people, I have seen that anyone can achieve his potential if he has the right approach.

G-d created every human being in His image. That means that no one is worthless. If G-d gives us life, and we are walking around in His world, there is surely a good reason for it: There is something important for us to accomplish, and we certainly have the ability to do so. So let's get started — now!

Even if we have let many years go by without achieving real purpose or creative activity, even if we feel that we have messed everything up, as long as we are alive and breathing we haven't missed the boat!

No one knows how much time he has left in this world; even young people have no way of knowing. We are all flesh and blood, here one day, gone the next. But one thing is certain: **Today is the beginning of the rest of your life.**

No matter what happened up until now, let us start today to get the most out of life!

If a person were to learn that he had only six months left to live, would he spend this short time trying to please or imitate others? Would he waste his time with fantasies, or would he do what he truly wants, what he thinks is correct, and what he knows might be possible?

Why wait for such a sad situation to occur?

Why think *If only?* **It's never too late. And it's never too soon.**

Success is not limited to any specific realm. If you learn how to succeed, you will succeed at whatever you work on, whether it's studying Torah or making money, improving a character trait or developing a talent, raising your status or parenting your children.

Many people don't feel successful in serving G-d. They fall into despair — and from there it's a short route to chucking the whole thing. "Sadness is not a sin," said R' Aharon of Karlin, "but what sadness can lead to, the worst sin cannot." If you learn how to be successful, you will also succeed in serving G-d with joy.

While reading this book, you will come to the happy realization that all of us can succeed in developing our talents and fulfilling our goals, if only we will adopt the right attitude and learn the proper way to do so. But improvement involves change. Learning to succeed may require changing some of your thinking and some of your actions.

To make my point, I will sketch extreme cases where people have gotten caught in a trap of their own making. You might identify one of them as your neighbor. If so, perhaps I have caused you some satisfaction. Perhaps you will even recommend that your neighbor read this book.

But that is not my purpose.

In each of us there is a little madman, perhaps even two or more. So when you see one of these sketches, ask yourself:

- Don't I resemble that person, even slightly, at least sometimes?
- Isn't there a smidgen of his frustration in me?
- Isn't it worthwhile for me to work on the little madman in me so that I won't become like the person in the sketch?

What Is Success?

We all want to succeed in life. Everyone in his right mind seeks fulfillment and self-esteem. We all want to feel good about ourselves, justify our existence, and value our deeds. Naturally, we put a lot of thought into how to succeed.

In striving for success, we must first define what we are after. Otherwise, we may find out when we reach our goal that what we had thought was success is actually failure.

What do we mean by "success"? By what yardstick do we measure it? What grade do we consider passing?

Aaron and Ben got back their math tests and looked at their marks.

Aaron's face lit up with joy. He stood up straight and tall and hummed a little tune to himself. He had passed — and with five points to spare!

Ben's head hung down and his shoulders drooped. He was disappointed and defeated. All he had gotten was 90.

Success is subjective. One man's triumph is another man's defeat.

What determines whether we rate something as success or failure?

M ath was Aaron's weakest subject. Although he had worked hard to keep up with the class, his previous marks had ranged between 30 and 50. For Aaron, passing was a dream. And now, this dream had come true.

For Ben, math was a cinch. He was used to getting 100 without even studying. Now he had dropped down 10 points and lost his place at the top of the class.

"Success" can be a 70 while "failure" can be a 90, depending on our expectations.

C laire and Dora both decided to open gift shops. Each woman rented a store, decorated it tastefully, and stocked it with quality merchandise that was priced to sell.

Claire, who thought she understood business, calculated that her shop would net $7,000 in monthly profits right from the start. She was crushed when the first month's profit turned out to be a mere $3,000.

Dora was advised that it takes time to build up a clientele and that she would be lucky to break even the first quarter. She was elated when the accounts showed a $2,000 profit for the opening month.

What makes $3,000 a failure and $2,000 a success is our expectation.

This holds true for every realm of life: social, political, personal, economic — you name it.

*E*dna, holding the baby on her lap, looked around the table at her children's shining faces as they waited eagerly for their father to make Kiddush on Friday night. What a pleasure to see them scrubbed and clean in their Shabbos best. A lot of work had gone into getting everything and everybody ready, but what a feeling of satisfaction now that it was all done! The challahs peeking out from under their embroidered cover seemed to wink at her. Thank heaven for the kosher grocery store down the block, where challahs and cake are sold for Shabbos. At least those two time-consuming tasks had been scratched off the to-do list.

Fradel, holding the baby on her lap, was almost embarrassed to look at her children's shining faces as they waited eagerly for their father to make Kiddush on Friday night. A lot of work had gone into getting everything and everybody ready, and now that it was done, she had little to show for her efforts. The challahs peeking out from under their embroidered cover seemed to mock her. Store-bought challahs and cake for Shabbos — two undeniable proofs of her failure as a housewife.

In addition to expectations, our values, too, determine what we perceive as success or failure.

*T*o Al Bloom, success was spelled "M.D." or "Ph.D." When he didn't earn the title, he was devastated. He was a dropout! He went to work in his uncle's export business and eventually opened his own branch. Today he earns ten times what he would have *earned with the coveted degrees, but still considers himself a failure.*

Carl Drucker's ambition in life was to have a successful business. He went to college like all his friends, but he was only biding his time until he could start his own business. He finished college and still the opportunity hadn't come along, so he continued along toward higher degrees. Today Professor Drucker has a comfortable position in a university, but feels he missed the boat.

Success is in the eyes of the viewer. It's a matter of perspective, determined by one's values and expectations.

If you are not as successful as you would like to be, it may be simply because you have unrealistic expectations. As a first step toward success, ask yourself:

- What are my expectations?
- Have I set them too high?
- Are they appropriate for me?

You may have been expecting the impossible of yourself. If you find yourself thinking a lot in terms of "should" — "I *should* be this" or "I *should* do that" — most likely you're driving up the wrong road. Adjust your expectations to fit reality. If you do, you will probably find that you are already more successful than you thought.

Even when you can't determine circumstances or the outcome of your efforts, you *can* control the degree of success you enjoy, simply by adjusting your expectations. The rosy new perspective you acquire will impact favorably on all the events in your life.

Before we actually define success, let's take a look at expectations (Chapter 3) and dreams (Chapter 4).

Check Your
Expectations

Each individual has his own unique personality, made up of a collection of character traits, personal views, and styles of relating. Without realizing it, we are constantly amassing data about people's personalities, which we automatically process and use to predict their reactions.

*S*am knows Michael to be a refined, stable man with strong self-control. Someone told Sam that Michael had beaten up a teenager for denting his new car. "Ridiculous!" said Sam. "I know Michael. He would never do such a thing!"

We use the very same tools to evaluate our own behavior. True, when it comes to ourselves, the margin of error is much larger. It is said that each person has three personalities: who he really is, who he thinks he is, and what he would like others to think he is. Nevertheless, we do develop a self-image. Before taking any action, we use our self-image to predict the consequences. We "know" in advance whether the action is appropriate for us. We also "know" what others will think of us for doing it; in our mind's eye, we already see them raising a quizzical eyebrow or enthusiastically cheering us on.

Our self-image strongly influences our opinions and expectations of ourselves and determines what goals we choose to pursue and by what means. It dictates how we relate to our virtues and faults, and how we measure our achievements.

This brings us to the next question: Where does our self-image come from?

During a child's formative years, a sensitive internal tape recorder picks up the opinions people have of him. He hears that he's smart or stupid, lovable or unbearable, good natured or nasty, quick or slow. In addition to opinion messages, there are also expectation messages. Parents, teachers, and even society at large inculcate in him the obligation to study Torah, serve Hashem, acquire wealth, pursue honor, and be an upright citizen. They encourage him by saying, "What a sharp answer! You're going to be a big *talmid chacham,*" or "With a mind like yours, you'll make it big in business." Or they discourage him by saying, "You never do anything right," "You have two left hands," or "You'll never amount to anything."

Every child receives opinion and expectation messages morning, noon, and night. He interprets them according to what he already believes and thinks about himself and, based on his interpretation, he gradually formulates an identity. His own interpretation will be the tape that he'll replay, again and again.

As this tape is replayed over the years, he internalizes its messages. Gradually he undertakes to play the role the tape outlines for him. He visualizes himself reaching the goal it chose for him. He will forge determinedly ahead in that direction and take all necessary steps to get there. He will try to project the self-image he has developed and to behave in a way consistent with it. He knows that if he doesn't, he will be considered strange; "people" will make fun of him. Even worse, *he* may conclude that something is wrong with him!

If the tape is negative, he will be convinced that this is how he really is, and he will behave accordingly. He won't work hard to succeed. Why bother? He already "knows" that he will fail.

All of us are actors guided by a script that consists of our interpretation of the messages we received from parents or society. This script, with its accompanying expectations, strongly affects our ability to reach fulfillment in life.

The Wrong Script

Sometimes the script is unsuitable. If it is, and we follow it blindly, the results can be devastating.

Daniel, a soft-spoken 18-year-old with many loyal friends, was respected for his fine character and admired for his scholastic achievements. Yet, he confided, he was acutely dissatisfied with himself. At times, feelings of inadequacy overwhelmed him to the point where he couldn't function. During the High Holidays, for instance, he had not been able to enter the synagogue; he simply felt too ashamed. Daniel had no idea where these destructive feelings were coming from.

I asked him about his childhood, and learned that Daniel was the only son of Kalman Silver, a lively extrovert with dazzling conversational skills. Whenever people got together, Kalman Silver was the center of attention, spouting interesting anecdotes and witty comments, holding his listeners spellbound.

As Daniel grew up, it became apparent that he was different from his father. He was a good boy who did well in school and had nice friends — but for Kalman Silver that wasn't enough. The father kept pushing his son to stand out in the crowd and develop the same social skills that he had – without success.

Occasionally, Daniel's teachers would point out that he was different from his father. Such "innocent" comments as "You're not going to be another Kalman Silver" implanted the feeling that he had missed the mark.

Daniel had come to study in Israel — where he was warmly welcomed by his father's old buddies. They spoke with nostalgia about Kalman Silver's charm, which had been striking even in his youth. One of them even wondered aloud whether Daniel was like his father.

In his new environment, Daniel became an out-standing student who was extremely considerate of others. But any time he ran into someone who "did him a favor" by telling him about his father, he became agitated. When a family friend visiting Israel brought him regards from home, Daniel waited like a compressed spring for the comments to hit.

The sporadic fire during the course of the year turned into a raging battle in the autumn, when many friends of the family came to Israel for the holidays. Merely seeing them reminded Daniel that he had fallen short of everyone's expectations. He was sure they were all looking at him askance.

Once we got to the root of the problem, I was able to help Daniel understand that he was under no obligation to emulate his father; moreover, there was no valid basis for any such expectation. The deadly germs of failure festering inside him had almost killed the sense of self he had worked so hard to develop.

Once his self-confidence was restored, his peace of mind returned. He was even able to meet his father's acquaintances with equanimity.

Daniel was following a script that said he was expected to be like his father. Unfortunately, Daniel's story is not unique. In the course of my work, I have encountered many successful people who felt bitterly dissatisfied with themselves without justifiable reason, only because they were following unsuitable scripts.

The Other Side of the Coin

The coin of programmed self-image has a flip side. Some children deliberately rebel and write a script that is exactly the opposite of what is expected of them. This may happen if parents or teachers pressure a small child into something that goes completely against his grain — for instance, if a parent forces a child to study while all his friends are outside playing. It may also happen if the child is disgusted by his parents' approach or embarrassed by his parents' behavior, or if society expects from him something he thinks is improper. In such cases, the child is liable to develop hatred and to rebel the moment he feels he has the power to do so. He will act according to a script completely opposite of the one they tried to write for him. He'll show them that *he'll* do what *he* wants.

Shmuel, who came from a family of renowned Torah scholars, confided that he had decided not to follow in his father's footsteps. He was leaving yeshivah and going to study law. He had developed an intense hatred for Torah scholars — a hatred that puzzled and disturbed even Shmuel himself.

In our sessions together, we discussed Shmuel's childhood. What emerged was that Shmuel's father led *a double life. In the community, he was a dignified, well-known rabbi. But at home his behavior was far from respectable.*

Shmuel's teachers, unaware of the dichotomy in the father's behavior, encouraged the child to study Torah diligently so that "when you grow up, you'll be like your father." Everyone else he knew sent him constant messages to the same effect. Little did they know that with every comment, they were pushing him further away from Torah study. Each "encouraging word" injected him with another dose of hatred for all that his father stood for. The words themselves disgusted Shmuel and made him view the world as a place of vanity and falsehood. He bided his time until the day he could rebel openly against his father and his environment.

Shmuel's story is an extreme, though not isolated, example. All of us are actors who follow a script that is based on the self-image we have developed and the values we have accepted or against which we have rebelled. This script, whether positive or negative, guides our actions.

The Right Script for You

When our accomplishments fall short of those in a positive script, even if objectively we are doing well, we still consider ourselves inadequate — because "more is expected of us."

If you follow a script that is wrong for your personality, you will waste time and energy and deplete your material, physical, and emotional resources. Playing an unsuitable role leads to failure.

This explanation of scripts, or any other explanation in this book, is no excuse for sitting around bemoaning our fate or flagellating ourselves. It is meant to show what we need to work on. As children, we may have been unable to defend ourselves from destructive messages, but now that we are adults, the responsibility for changing is ours alone. We have to take ourselves in hand and pull ourselves out of the darkness.

Begin by asking yourself:

- What taped messages are playing in my mind?
- What expectations am I trying to fulfill?
- What script am I following?

The understanding you gain can save you much frustration and anguish.

Make sure the script you are following is suitable for you.

Your own dreams may be quite different from the ones in the script. Let's take a look at dreams.

Dare to Dream

All of us have fantasies about what we would like to accomplish. In fact, dreams are the beginning of all great achievements.

As a young man, Henry Ford spent his spare time building a gasoline-powered automobile. When he finished it, in 1896, the car looked like a wooden box on bicycle tires. It only went forward and it used an electric doorbell for a horn — but it ran.

Ford kept working on his car — improving it, rebuilding it, and showing it to people. He also worked on saving time and money manufacturing it. Initially each car was built separately. Because it took a long time to build, it was so expensive that only the rich could buy one. Ford dreamed of building a car that the average person could afford. He improved the assembly line and made it work. His engineers tested different ways of cutting production time. In

1907, it took 12½ hours to made the Model T; by 1914, it took only 1½. Cutting production time and increasing volume led to dramatic reductions in cost. Ford was able to offer more cars to the American public at a lower price than anyone before him.

Ford had a dream, and he took steps to transform it into reality. The question we have to ask ourselves is: What must we do to realize our dream?

*T*he eyes of Saul Levy, janitor, shone with joy as he vividly described the wealthy, successful businessman he would become. Everyone in the community would look at him with envy; no one would dare make a move without first securing his consent. But that was not enough. He would become famous and influential throughout the Jewish world. "When I pass by in the street," he told me, "everyone will turn around and point. 'There goes the great philanthropist, Mr. Saul Levy.' "

The status he described was modest enough, considering the list of institutions that he promised to support and the sums of money he was going to put into every outstretched palm.

Then I asked, "What are you doing to turn your dream into reality?"

He looked at me as if I had awoken him from a deep sleep. "What can I do?" he said miserably.

But after a few seconds, he recovered his composure. "Just wait," he assured me. "You'll see."

One day Saul told me that he had started taking action: He was sending himself letters! He had also ordered advertising brochures from various companies. The large quantities of mail that arrived at his house were sure to impress the mailman delivering them.

But the mailman was not the only who would be impressed. The fame of Saul Levy would spread throughout the land.

Saul's efforts paid off. His name and address found their way onto computerized mailing lists. He was deluged with advertisements and requests for donations. Even political parties sent him mail before elections.

Don't laugh. Saul Levy is not alone in his dreams. There are many more like him who are embarrassed to admit it.

Myself, for instance. But for the sake of helping others, I will admit it.

I grew up in New York and went to study in Jerusalem, where I met my wife. Since she came from Brazil, we moved there two months after our wedding.

Even though Brazil is the world's fifth largest country, to me, its people and its climate were strange and different. I sorely missed the large, thriving Jewish communities of which I had always been part. The isolation and loneliness were painful, the boredom frightening. I wanted desperately to leave, but lacked the means to do so.

Out of boredom, I began to make calculations on my pocket calculator. One day I wondered: If I had $100 million, how much would it bring me in dividends over the course of a year? Almost on their own, my fingers began to enter the figures. The results were astonishing. No matter what percent interest I used, I still came out with more than enough to support all my grandchildren and their descendants for many generations, even without touching the principal. I was in the clouds.

After a while, a new idea occurred to me. My friendly calculator could process up to 12 digit numbers. Why begin with only 100 million? Why not go for the maximum: $999,999,999,999? Enthusiastically I began my calculations from the beginning. What pleasure I had in seeing the amazing sums I would earn yearly!

The little calculator gave me many hours of bliss. Then, one day when I picked it up, it didn't respond to my fingers. The battery had died. All that was left of my dreams was a silent instrument.

I could easily have bought a new battery. But suddenly I realized that I had been wasting many hours on nonsense. All my calculations added up to a grand total of 12 times zero.

That is the end of all dreams — if action does not accompany them.

I learned my lesson and took action. I borrowed money and moved back to Jerusalem.

To be successful, we need to work on transforming our dream into reality.

Wish Versus Will

Even if our dream is more modest than Saul Levy's, we still need to chart a course and take concrete steps to turn it into reality.

> **"F**or years I've wanted to sell computers," Morris told me. "I have friends who've gone into the field and prospered."
>
> "And what have you done about it?" I asked him. "Have you applied to a distributor for a job in order to learn the ropes? Have you gotten information?"
>
> No, he hadn't.

"Where there's a will, there's a way," doesn't apply to people like Morris, who have only a wish, but not a will.

What's the difference between "wish" and "will"?

Wish means that I hope in my heart something will happen. "If only I would win the lottery" is a wish; there is nothing I myself can do to achieve my desire. Of such things, the blessing "May Hashem fulfill all your wishes for the good," is appropriate since only He can do something about them.

Will is expressed in a deed that I am about to do in order to materialize my desire. If I truly desire to attain something and can do something about it, I won't say, "If only," but rather "I will." Let's say I run out of milk. If I have the ability to go to the grocery store and buy milk, I won't say, "If only I could go." I will get up and go. But if I can't go because the store is closed, "If only I could go" makes sense.

We all have dreams. But what are we doing to make them come true? If we want a dream to materialize, we must switch from wish to will. We must plan a course of action, roll up our sleeves, and get down to work. Then, "where there's a will, there's a way."

"Believe me, I so much want to learn Torah," Tzvi told me. "But it just doesn't go."*

The beis midrash is open and the sefarim are available. Why, then, does Tzvi choose not to go in? Is something preventing him from sitting down to study?

Tzvi has the wish to sit and study, but not the will. He wants to want to study; he doesn't have enough desire to invest the effort it takes to fulfill his wish.

Dreams, sweet as they may be, will not bring you closer to your goal — unless, when you wake up from your reverie, you invest effort in making them come true. Many people invest too much in dreaming and planning and not enough in doing.

If you want to build a new house, of course you must first visualize what the house will look like and plan it out in detail. But then the real work begins — hard, backbreaking labor. Only after several weeks of digging up the earth can you begin the actual process of building. It is impossible to put on the roof before you have built the walls, and you can't finish the walls without laying the first row of bricks.

To make progress, you have to start from the bottom and build up. No one has yet managed to get to the top of the ladder without lifting his foot up to the first rung.

Every king, general, and revolutionary leader without exception was born naked and helpless. This is the starting point of each of us. The difference is what we do from then on.

Dreams are only the beginning. The actions that follow them are what determine whether they will become reality or remain forever in the realm of fantasy. "There are some people who live in a dream world, and there are some who face reality; and then there are those who turn one into the other" (Douglas Everett).

Set Goals

To help us start converting our dreams into reality, I would like to suggest the following definition:

Success is reaching your goal.

This definition has implications. In order to reach your goal, you must first have one. That is, you must clearly delineate a goal that you want to reach. Taking action to reach this goal will bring you satisfaction, fulfillment, and success.

Why is setting a goal so important?

From a young age, we develop a desire to be special and to excel in some area. Here and there we see successful people, and the natural, healthy jealousy[1] that the Creator implanted in us spurs us on to master some field of endeavor.

---

1. Any emotion can be positive or negative, depending on what you do with it.

Jealousy is positive when you use it to motivate yourself to reach a higher goal — not because you can't stand that Reuven is better than you (in which case you would stop trying if Reuven failed), but because having seen that the goal is attainable, you want to get there, too. In this case, "Jealousy of scholars increases wisdom" (*Bava Basra* 21a).

Jealousy is negative when you are unhappy about Reuven's success and try to hurt him or make him lose what he has won. This destructive kind of jealousy is called *tzarus ayin.*

But as information pours in from all directions, our horizons broaden, our possibilities increase — and so does our confusion.

A likely result is that our ambitions will keep changing. One day we will want to be a rabbi, the next a lawyer; one day to be in the limelight, the next to keep out of the public eye. We will jump from one thing to another — a sure way to accumulate disappointments and feel we're getting nowhere. Our self-confidence will be eroded.

"This world is like a corridor before the World to Come. Prepare yourself in the corridor so that you can enter the palace" (*Avos* 4:21). When you walk through a corridor, you're moving along from one point to another. The corridor is not an end in itself, but a means of coming closer to the palace. But in order to get to the palace, you must know which corridor to use and in which direction to go. How can you keep on going if you don't know whether you're headed in the right direction?

Indeed, sometimes confusion about goals leads to doing nothing. This happens when people think that if they had been born with different traits, they would have achieved great things — the things they *really* want.

Mr. Taub, known in his community as responsible, intelligent, and capable, came to me to find out what he could do to succeed in life. He was a talented fellow — he told me so himself — but he didn't know what field to choose. He did nothing in life except go to various psychologists and advisers to find out what field suited him.

In the course of the session, I found out that he was acutely jealous of the successful people around him. He consoled himself with the thought that if he were to do what they did, he would outshine them. In his eyes, it was a pity to choose one specific field;

*there was always another field in which he could
work less and succeed more.*

Mr. Taub reminds me of the immigrant who came to the United States in the old days, when the streets were reputedly paved with money. The relatives who turned out to greet him in the New York harbor noticed a $20 bill at his feet. "Pick it up," they urged.

"Why bother picking up a 20," said the immigrant, "when there are $100 bills rolling around the city?"

Progress is impossible without a clearly defined goal. Knowing where you're going enables you to take resolute action and to work in a single direction consistently and methodically toward success.

Setting goals is important for another reason as well. Goals give life meaning.

When Meaning Is Missing

Life is a journey. Someone who sets out without a defined goal can travel miles and miles without coming any closer to his destination — because he has none. It makes no difference to him whether he sails east or west. In his eyes, tomorrow is the same as yesterday, with only the seasons and his age changing. He goes through life without knowing what he wants out of it, drifting wherever circumstance sends him like a bottle afloat in the ocean. His whole life consists of bits and pieces that don't add up to anything. He exists, but is not living in the full sense of the word. He is on a treadmill, moving and working and getting nowhere.

It's not surprising, then, if he feels that he is no more than another grain of sand on the seashore or another drop of water in the ocean, whose presence doesn't contribute anything and whose absence will not be felt. No wonder he is bored and frustrated.

"What's happening to me?" asked Mr. Saltz, a middle-aged man with sad eyes. "Why do I feel dissatisfied and unhappy? It doesn't make sense. Thank G-d, we are all healthy. I work hard but earn a good living; I keep the mitzvos. And yet, I feel so empty."

I asked him to tell me about his daily schedule. "It runs like clockwork," said Mr. Saltz. "I get up in the morning, daven Shacharis in the local shul, come home and eat breakfast, go to work, come home tired, eat supper, go back to shul for Minchah and Maariv, participate in the daily shiur, chat a bit with my friends, come home, and go to sleep. Day in, day out."

After this description, Mr. Saltz already understood the problem himself, and asked, "How do you put a little joy into such a life?"

Many people, old and young, feel like Mr. Saltz when they get locked into a fixed daily routine. This is often true of yeshivah students, who are on a strict schedule from the minute they wake up to the minute they go to sleep. But it also happens to those people whose lives look vibrant and interesting to the outside world; they too sometimes suffer from the thought, "For what am I toiling? I work from morning to night, and what do I get out of it all?"

In my work I have seen that many people whose lives are joyless have no defined goal. They can't answer the question, "Where am I going?"

The Need for Meaning

Goals give meaning to our lives. And finding meaning is one of the secrets of our existence.

Having a goal that is meaningful *to you* makes you willing to invest the effort and pay the price to reach it. The more meaningful the goal is to you, the higher the price you will be willing to pay.

This principle extends beyond working toward a goal; it encompasses our general ability to cope with the vicissitudes of life.

Even under the best circumstances, life is full of troubles. Finding meaning in his suffering enables a person to deal courageously with his troubles instead of being overwhelmed by them. It bolsters the spirit and banishes despair. The greater the meaning is in his eyes, the more he will be willing to "pay."

Tzaddikim have undertaken fasts and afflictions to atone for themselves and others. Jewish history is replete with heroes who would not renounce their faith even in the face of torture and death. Revolutionaries have endured dozens of years in solitary confinement for their cause.

As a psychologist, Dr. Victor Frankl asked deeply troubled people, "Why don't you commit suicide?" Invariably the answer was that they had something or someone to live for. As a concentration camp inmate, Frankl observed that those who saw some meaning or purpose in survival managed to endure the unimaginable horrors, while those who did not, quickly succumbed. Based on his findings, he developed logotherapy, which helps people find meaning in their lives.

"Emotional problems arise from being purposeless," said Frankl. "Mental health is based on the tension between what you are and what you think you should become. You should be striving for worthy goals" (Frankl, *Man's Search for Meaning*).

Dr. Bernie Siegel noticed that his patients recovered almost miraculously from serious illnesses if they found meaning in their lives and began working to accomplish new goals. Siegel left his job as a surgeon and began running support groups to help the seriously ill (Siegel, *Love, Medicine, and Miracles*)

My father suffered from cancer for four and a half years. The tumor spread to the point *where it blocked the large intestine. A bypass was necessary — but the doctors put it off as long as possible, saying there was no chance for him to come out of the operating room alive. They waited for him to die, but he didn't. Three weeks before my wedding, they decided the operation could not be postponed any longer.*

As the youngest and only unmarried child, I spent the night before the operation in the hospital with my father. He knew what the doctors had said, but he told me, "Don't worry. You'll see, with Hashem's help I will live and I won't spoil your wedding."

Contrary to predictions, he survived the operation. They sent him home three weeks later — on my wedding day. He was not well, but he was alive. He was brought to the chupah, recited a blessing, and was taken home.

On the last evening of the week of Sheva Berachos, my father had an attack and returned to the hospital. He died six weeks later.

My father had a goal — not to spoil my wedding — and that goal pulled him through.

Having a goal not only strengthens the spirit; it spurs people into action. Mothers have run into burning houses to save their children. Demagogues have gotten people to risk their lives by stirring up zealousness for a cause. On the other hand, a person who lacks purpose will feel listless and is liable to fall into depression. If someone complains of boredom and emptiness, it is a clear sign that he does not *feel* there is purpose, even if he knows it intellectually.

To derive satisfaction from life, put some meaning into it by setting up a worthwhile, suitable goal that you will strive to attain. With your goal clearly in mind, you can invest effort and energy in a defined direction and work consistently toward it. Then you will be able to answer these questions:

- In what ways is my situation today significantly different from what it was a month ago?
- How will my life be different a month from now?
- Where do I crave to go in life?

When you have a goal, you will feel a sense of accomplishment. You will lead a happy life, full of satisfaction and meaning.

Choosing a Goal

What goal should you choose?

The ancient prophets of Israel could have answered that question for you. They were able to tell a person why he was created and what he had to do to succeed (*Beur HaGra* on the verse "Everything Hashem made [He made] for His sake" — *Mishlei* 16:4). But very few people today can tell you what is right for you. Certainly no book can answer this question. Since each person is unique, there is an individual answer for each one.

But we *can* discuss how to go about choosing a goal.

Get acquainted with yourself. Only you can know what interests and excites you; and only reaching a goal that you are excited about will bring you fulfillment. I have met many people who studied computers, only to drop out in the middle or work in a different field after finishing. It's the old eyeglasses mistake: Just because I see clearly through my glasses doesn't mean that you will. The computer dropouts had been pursuing a goal that others told them was worthwhile, rather than one that they themselves truly desired.

What goal, then, should you choose? The answers are right there, inside you; it's up to you to dig in and find them. That may take a lot of effort. Sometimes years of searching go into finding the avenue that truly satisfies a person's soul. The better you know yourself, the greater your chances of succeeding in the end.

Focus on discovering your natural talents and strong points so that you can build on them. You can only build on what you have, not on what you lack. Note your weaknesses in order to see what goals to avoid.

Ask yourself honestly:
- What talents has G-d granted me?
- How can I use them in the best possible way?
- What do I want to achieve in life?
- How do I plan to get there?
- What am I aiming for at this stage?

Record your answers on paper. Do your answers to the last three questions correlate with your answers to the first two questions? If not, you may be trying to achieve something that is not realistic for you at this point.

Setting realistic goals is not easy. Often our understanding of ourselves is mistaken. We don't know the true "me." In searching for suitable goals that match our various needs, we must distinguish between truth and fantasy, between what we really want and what we were taught we "must" want. The more deeply we think, the greater our chances of doing the right thing for the right reason.

It is said that a wise person recognizes his place. A person must know himself and set his goals accordingly.

Talents and abilities go further than being artistic, musical, athletic, or scholarly. Do you prefer working alone or with other people? With machines, books, or animals? Leadership, organizational or speaking skills, getting along with others, and the ability to study independently or withstand criticism are but a few of the qualities that should be considered. Each of us must choose a goal that is appropriate for us.

Freedom of Choice

Each person has the right, and even the obligation, to choose what suits him (as long, of course, as it does not negate the commands of the Torah and our rabbis). No one can force you to pursue a goal that is not comfortable for you.

Just as no one can argue that I should like the food that he likes or wear shoes his size (although that size is very comfortable for him), so no one has the right to argue that I should aim for the same goal he does.

Other people have the right to think differently from me, even to think that I am mistaken. But by the very same token, I have the right to think differently from him! Each person must search his own soul and follow his own conscience.

Some are afraid of this view lest their children choose a goal that goes contrary to the Torah. But this is akin to forcing their children to stay home so they won't go to forbidden places, or blindfolding them so they won't look at forbidden sights. We can't use force or threats; we must educate children to do what is proper. With intelligence and wisdom, we must teach our children to take responsibility for their actions and to live with self-discipline. And as they mature, we must encourage them to choose their own goals, in accordance with the Torah, even if the goals they choose are not exactly what we like.

Those who enter into a certain field of study or work to please their parents are liable to be irritable and miserable, which will naturally impact on their marriage as well. Many talented people have missed the boat only because they tried to adopt someone else's goal. Whoever chooses a goal that doesn't suit him may possibly sow with joy but will certainly reap with tears. The only way to succeed is by pursuing a goal that is right for you.

On the other hand, make sure your goal does not conflict with the accepted norms of your surroundings, or you're liable to lose more than you gain. Don't solve your financial problems by becoming a clown if that will mortify your wife and children. In the language of neurolinguistic programming (NLP), look for an ecological solution — a solution consonant with your environment.

From Goals to Action

Once you have chosen a goal, define it as concretely and clearly as possible. If your answer to what you want to achieve in life was "find fulfillment," sit down and think: *What specific things will give me fulfillment?* Setting up a vague, general goal is like packing your suitcase and leaving your house to go on a two-week vacation "somewhere."

After defining your goal, map out the road you will take to reach it. Prepare a practical plan of action. List the steps in as much detail as possible so that you can progress methodically, step by step, and check off each item as you accomplish it.

Set a date for reaching your goal. If the destination is too far in the distance, the mission will seem impossible. Break down your long-term goal into smaller sub-goals, each with its own deadline. Split tasks into sub-tasks, even if they need to be done simultaneously. If you work in stages, you will feel progress with every step.

Schedule breaks and vacations for the purpose of replenishing your strength.

Set dates for evaluating results. Don't evaluate prematurely! (More on that in Chapter 11.)

For instance, the Youngs have always dreamed of moving to Israel, and now they want to make the move. They have broken the project into two stages. In January, they will make a pilot trip to find: (1) work, (2) a place to live, and (3) schools for the children. If this trip is successful, they will allot six months to: (1) sell the house, (2) decide what to do with their various belongings (sell, give away, ship, take along), and (3) pack. Their goal is to move in August, before the new school year starts.

A man who wants to learn the entire Talmud is more likely to succeed if he assigns a date for completing the project; breaks this goal down into smaller sub-goals (completing tractates), each with its own date; and then decides how many pages he wants to cover each week and each day. That way, if he misses a few hours in the course of the week, he will be able to make them up. Even when there are deviations, he will remain within a defined framework.

Making Pesach is much simpler if you break the major goal into sub-tasks: cleaning the various rooms of the house, buying clothes, shopping for food, cooking for the holiday. Assign a date by which each sub-task must be finished. Then break it down further.

Checking off items on your to-do list is very satisfying. Dividing your major goal into much smaller ones will give you a sense of fulfillment each day. You'll go to sleep at night feeling that you are closer to your goal than when you woke up in the morning. The sense of accomplishment will act as a stimulus to keep you moving forward.

Reevaluate

From time to time, review your goals to see whether they suit your present situation. As you progress and acquire new skills, you may be able to set higher goals.

That's what Wilma Rudolph did. She was the twentieth child of a poor African-American family in Tennessee. Underweight and sickly as a baby, she contracted pneumonia, scarlet fever, and then polio, which paralyzed her legs.

Wilma's first goal was to walk. Finally, at the age of 8, she began walking with the help of a leg brace. By 11 she was playing basketball. Then she set herself a higher goal: to run. She exercised regularly, and by the age of 13 she had strong, normal legs. She won every running contest in high school and became an All-State basketball player.

As her abilities improved, Wilma reevaluated her goals and raised them. With the aim of becoming the country's best woman runner, she trained for the Olympics. In 1960, she broke the Olympic record for the 100- and 200-meter dash, and her team won the 400-meter relay race. Wilma became the first American woman to win three gold medals during the same Olympics.

"Consider three things and you will not come to sin. Know from where you have come, where you are going, and before Whom you will give reckoning" (*Avos* 3:1). "Know from where you have come" — take stock of your situation today; and know "where you are going" — what your goals are. Each person was sent into this world to carry out a certain unique mission. To succeed at yours, you need to keep on assessing your situation and setting higher and higher goals so that you draw continually closer to G-d. In this way, you will always see a difference between yesterday and today. You will work energetically to progress, at your own pace, toward the goal of meeting your Creator.

Where Is Happiness?

We have seen that a goal needs to be more specific than just "achieve happiness." But whatever our clearly defined goal is, we hope that it will bring us happiness, satisfaction, and fulfillment.

What is happiness, and how do we find it?

Once upon a time, a king became depressed. He consulted an expert physician. "The only remedy," pronounced the physician, "is for Your Majesty to wear the shirt of a happy man."

The king's servants went out in search of a happy man. They started looking among the rich. But they soon discovered that the rich were so preoccupied with their businesses and their investments that they could not enjoy their wealth.

Then the king's servants searched among the middle class. Here, too, they did not find a happy man. They *learned that the middle class was preoccupied with trying unsuccessfully to be like the rich.*

After the king's servants had given up on finding a happy person, they passed by a hovel and heard someone singing. They said, "Surely a happy person must live here." They went in and saw that they were right.

"Yes, I am happy," proclaimed the destitute man. "But I don't have a shirt."

Many people seek happiness and don't find it. Evidently they don't know exactly what they're looking for. They have actually confused momentary pleasure with lasting happiness.

Satisfying our material or physical desires is like getting a fat check written in disappearing ink. Before long, the delight vanishes into thin air. Not for nothing is it called "satisfying one's passions." The person who gives in to his desire satisfies his passion, but not himself — not his inner "I."

Some think that if only they were rich, they would be full of joy until their dying day. Reality proves otherwise. Research studies showed that lottery winners who had been bitter, angry, or frustrated before they won millions of dollars continued to be bitter, angry, or frustrated afterward. People stay the same.

So does civilization in general. Technology has revolutionized every area of life, raised the standard of living, and made our work easier. But the problems of the human race remain as they were. Computers, cellular phones, microwave ovens, and e-mail correspondence have not increased the joy of living. Jealousy, lust, self-aggrandizement, and other bad traits did not die out together with the horse and buggy. People have stayed the same.

We all need some pleasure in life; almost everyone has a list of needs and wants: friendships, fun, a good sound system, a nice car, fine clothes. The problem starts when we begin to believe that pleasures and possessions will make us happy — because they can't. Friends drift away; power fades; houses deteriorate; clothes go out of style; cars break down, and there is always something newer, faster, bigger, or more expensive; old pleasures lose their thrill, and eating makes us fat.

Once we say, "If only I had X, I'd be happy," we've created a destructive mind game. If we get what we want, we're happy for a while — and then we become accustomed to it, and the boredom returns.

All of us go through many "If only" cycles.

Let's think back to our childhood. How many times were we ready to promise that if only our parents would buy us a certain toy, we would be happy forever? Yet a few days after we got what we wanted, we were back to our old whining. We did not acquire the magic source of happiness. The toy did not change reality by one iota.

This continues to happen throughout the course of life. When we studied in elementary school, we were convinced that when we became bar or bat mitzvah, we would be big, and everything would change. Then it was when we entered high school, college, yeshivah, seminary. Ah, when we get engaged — then surely all problems and troubles will belong to the past. After the wedding, we'll float permanently on cloud nine.

But always, after we became accustomed to our new situation, our previous state of mind returned in full force. The real "I," which remained intact, always surfaced.

Why?

Imagination

Imagination, by its very nature, has no limits. It is not bound by time, space, or any other parameters of reality. It travels with lightning speed. One moment you are a king living in a royal palace; the next, a beggar sleeping on a park bench. One moment you are in China; the next, on Mars. Past and future coexist. You can attend both King Solomon's dedication of the first Temple and the Messiah's dedication of the third. Freedom from the constraints of reality makes the imagination exciting and fruitful.

That is where our thoughts are — until they become realized. Then they become subject to nature and reality, which impose firm limits, at the cost of excitement.

Thus, "thoughts of sins are worse than sin itself" (*Yoma* 29a). As long as a person is thinking of sin, he imagines its pleasure in an exaggerated way. But when he actually commits the sin, the pleasure shrinks into the narrow bounds of reality.

That is why we are sure that if only such and such would happen, everything would be different. We imagine only one side of the coin, the side that makes us feel good. But life is complex. Alongside the good things, there are always hardships. When a person is swept away by imagination, he forgets that plenty of unpleasant things will still remain in his life. After our dream comes true, reality will take over and impose restrictions, leaving us disappointed.

Of course, G-d did not create imagination to taunt us. Imagination is the first step in any course of action, and the more fertile the imagination, the more productive the outcome can be. Every successful project or wonderful deed was first created in the imagination; that's where our ideas come from.

Nevertheless, we must remember that **imagination is not reality.**

Value

No external factor can lead us to true inner satisfaction and happiness. We can try to convince ourselves that all is well, but feelings don't lie. The emotional conscience is the soul's antenna. A person who feels dissatisfied won't succeed in repressing these feelings no matter how hard he tries. He may say — and think — that all is well at home and on the job, yet he doesn't feel happy. Even if he doesn't understand why, he will always be tormented by the feeling that something is missing.

> **A**s a teenager, Yossi left his religious family and all that they stood for. Speaking to me, he vented his wrath against his parents and teachers, who, he said, didn't understand him. At the same time, he repeated over and over, "Now I'm living it up. What freedom! It's a great life. I wouldn't return to the ghetto for a million dollars."
>
> "There's one thing I don't understand," I said. "If you're so happy, you should be grateful to your parents and teachers for pushing you into this wonderful situation. It's only thanks to them that you're living it up today!"
>
> He was silent for a moment. Then he gave me a look full of pain and humiliation. "Yeah," he said. "You and your wisecracks."

I've spoken to many youngsters like Yossi. Their anger gives them away. They know the truth: They lacked the strength of character to overcome their baser drives. They know that their arguments are only to assuage their consciences. They announce to the world that they're happy, but in private conversations they reveal their heartbreak. They do indeed blame their parents and teachers — for not knowing how to help them.

Happiness requires harmony between mind and heart. If the mind broadcasts one message, and the heart another, the heart's message will shake us up — and we will continue to search for something that we can't define.

Sometimes people do things that are opposed to their true inner will, whether because they are under the thumb of others or slaves to their own passions. In either case, find inner peace. Deep down inside, they will feel ᴇ degraded. As King Solomon said, "The heart know terness of its soul" (*Mishlei* 14:10).

Just as hand cream does not relieve the pain of a dᴇ so external things do not fill our deep inner needs. If ᴊ ᴜ are looking for happiness and fulfillment in an external source, you simply have the wrong address.

What, then, is the right address?

The true longing inside us is for esteem and honor — not so much from others as from ourselves. We yearn to feel that we are valuable human beings.

In order to find lasting happiness, we must do something of genuine value. Fake status symbols don't fool us. Inside ourselves, each of us is able to identify something of value when he does it.

Genuine satisfaction is caused by self-actualization. When a person does something that he feels has value and that he is proud of, he delights in his accomplishment, and this causes him tremendous satisfaction.

The more unique the deed is to him, the more potential there is for satisfaction. For instance, building a whole cabinet from scratch is more likely to produce satisfaction than standing on an assembly line and putting in a screw.

An act of value that brings satisfaction can be running a business or teaching first graders to read. It can be visiting a sick friend, studying Torah enthusiastically for an hour, saying a prayer with heartfelt fervor, or holding back a juicy piece of *lashon hara* that was at the tip of one's tongue.

A great source of bliss is helping the needy or cheering the brokenhearted. Some authorities claim that all it takes to get out of depression is to spend two hours a week doing acts of kindness for others.

The pleasure of past good deeds continues in the present. Take a second now to remember a good meal that you ate two years ago. Do you feel the pleasure now? Probably not. Now think back to one of your good deeds of the past. Doesn't the memory fill you with satisfaction? Inner feelings don't lie, and they show that doing good deeds makes people happy.

Any positive deed that *I do* — as opposed to something good that happened to me — brings joy and fulfillment. Any creative act that leaves me feeling that *I did* something important increases my self-esteem. Such acts never lose their value.

This is self-actualization.

So don't be surprised when the external factors on which we pinned our hopes don't lead us to happiness. What does lead there is creativity, self-actualization, behavior based on true values, and life full of content. What brings us satisfaction is not the good things that happen to us, but the good things that we ourselves do — because only these satisfy the soul's hunger for self-esteem.

Be Yourself

I n choosing a goal and pursuing it, make sure to **be true to yourself.**

> *J oe Smith — capable, talented, popular, and rich — was a leading figure in his community. One day Smith's neighbors were startled to see moving men carrying a Steinway grand piano into his house. "When did you start playing piano?" the neighbors asked.*
>
> *Smith winked at them. "You want to know the truth? I never learned to play. But yesterday I went to a concert and I watched the pianist. He didn't impress me as being particularly bright, yet his fingers flew effortlessly across the keys. If he could do it so easily, there is no reason that I, Joe Smith, shouldn't be able to!"*

We may smile to ourselves, but don't we, too, sometimes behave like Joe Smith? Aren't our actions sometimes based on Smith-type logic?

True, we should set up challenging goals for ourselves — even if the motivation is jealousy of someone else's achievements. Nothing is wrong with this; "jealousy of scholars increases wisdom" (*Bava Basra* 21a). Seeing a successful person motivates us to our own attainments. But to exactly imitate someone else's lifestyle or the means he used to achieve his success can be disastrous.

*M*eir was an excellent librarian — methodical, organized, and deliberate. He was also soft hearted and naive. His friend Shlomo, who was quick at making decisions and shrewd at sizing up people and situations, bought and sold apartment buildings. When Shlomo became rich, Meir's jealousy impelled him to follow in Shlomo's footsteps. He forgot to take into account the difference in their personalities.

When Meir first entered the business, there seemed to be many opportunities for profitable deals. But it wasn't long before an unscrupulous wheeler-dealer got him into deep financial trouble.

Meir's problem was not his naiveté, but his unawareness of it. Had he analyzed and understood his own personality, he would have realized that Shlomo's occupation would not be suitable for him.

I've seen people borrow money and invest heavily in stocks after So-and-so made a killing on Wall Street. The imitators lost their shirts because they, unlike So-and-so, didn't know the basics of investing.

The Blueprint of Creation

There are many people who would love to change places with someone else. The young are jealous of the old, the sharp-minded of the deep thinker, the practical of the man of ideas, and so on ad infinitum and vice versa. All of them think the neighbor's tools are more effective than theirs.

But trying to be a carbon copy of someone else goes against the very blueprint of creation.

No two people are identical. "Just as their faces are different, so are their minds" (*Tanchuma, Pinchas* 10). Even though the face is made up of only two eyes, one nose, and one mouth, arranged in a particular way, no two out of the world's six billion inhabitants have identical faces. The soul is infinitely more complex than the face; surely no two people have identical talents, minds, characters, and emotions. And no two people have the identical mission in life.

Baruch is by nature a quiet introvert who prefers the company of books to that of people. He sits and studies alone for hours on end without a break. Eliezer is a bubbly, dynamic extrovert. If Eliezer forces himself to behave like Baruch, he is setting himself up for failure.

To be complete, the earth needs mountains, valleys, jungles, deserts, rivers, and oceans. The year needs days of thanksgiving, days of repentance, days of holiness, and ordinary weekdays. The human body needs a heart, an appendix, blood, toes, skin, lungs, and earlobes. Mankind needs all different types of people. And each individual must fulfill his own unique mission for everything to work well.

Imagine a yeshivah where the cook deals with public relations, the secretary orders the *mashgiach* to use a certain approach that she thinks is beneficial, and the maintenance man fires a teacher because his *shiurim* aren't deep enough!

When G-d created each person in His image and assigned him a special mission in the world, He also furnished him with a wealth of talents and traits with which to accomplish it. Would the King of kings send someone here to fulfill a task without equipping him with the right tools for the job?

How could the world function if everyone used other people's tools?

Picture a construction site where the bricklayer, with his coarse equipment, tries to set up the electric wires; the electrician, with his delicate tools, attempts to dig the foundations; the carpenter, with his hammer and nails, sets out to lay the sewage pipes; and the crane operator intends to use his crane to install the windows.

When we see a friend succeeding in his task, we become jealous and want to do what he does — but we don't have the tools that he has!

If a short person walks around on tiptoe in order to look tall, he will probably hurt himself so that he won't even be able to walk normally. If someone tries to imitate others, not only won't he succeed in being like them, he won't even succeed in being what he could have been.

Don't imitate others. You'll never make it by trying to be what you are not; imitating others is a mission impossible with zero chance of success. So pray for the wisdom to recognize your strengths and be aware of your limitations. Develop your own tools wisely and fill the role that truly suits you. Then you will be able to successfully fulfill the mission for which you were sent into this world.

Imposters

Some people try to convince themselves that they have impressive traits by proclaiming how great they are. Once they become convinced of the truth of their own declarations, they try desperately to put substance into their words by taking on roles that don't match their abilities. They may undertake projects that they can't possibly get off the ground or demand that others treat them like royalty. Some lack a sense of responsibility yet struggle to become politicians who decide the public fate; others don't get along with people yet pretend to represent them all. They fail repeatedly and are rebuffed again and again. But instead of learning a lesson, they rant and rave against the wickedness of men who fail to recognize their amazing ability to contribute to society.

That is the best-case scenario. Sometimes these imposters succeed in convincing others of their dubious talents. The believers are pulled after them like sheep after a blind shepherd who doesn't see the abyss until it is too late.

The story is told of a dog who was tired of being chased by the village people and of having to burrow through the garbage in search of food. He wanted to be treated like a man. So he put on clothing and a mask. With head held high, he walked into the local inn.

It didn't take long for the people at the inn to notice the tail sticking out of his clothes. They beat up the disguised dog and threw him out.

Sore and hurt, the dog in men's clothing dragged himself to the pack of dogs outside the village. At least soon he would be among friends who would comfort him — or so he hoped.

The dogs, seeing a "man" walking toward them on all fours, attacked him with their sharp teeth.

Don't pretend to be what you're not. When someone pretends to be what he isn't, people eventually discover the lie and rebuff him. The wise will notice his stupidity; the stupid, his conceit; the ignorant, his hypocrisy. He won't fit into any group or find acceptance anywhere. Pitiful indeed.

How It Happened

What pushes so many people to want to be like someone else at all costs? Why don't they dare to be what they are?

The answer is that they were never taught to accept themselves! They may even have been brought up to think that they themselves are worthless, and their only hope is to imitate others.

Although Lazer is an intelligent young man of good character and outstanding scholarship, he could not see a single good quality in himself. He was full of guilt feelings and he felt powerless to do anything positive.

I asked Lazer what words of encouragement he used to hear from his parents. In response, he told me: "Often my father would say, 'Look at that boy. He's so nice! It's a pleasure speaking to him.' With undisguised pain he would add, 'Why can't you be like him?' Regardless of what I did, he always complained and was never satisfied with me."

With "encouragement" like that, it's not hard to understand why Lazer had developed a negative self-image.

Such parents want very much for their child to succeed. They don't realize that by educating their child to imitate others, they are teaching him that he himself is worthless.

If your parents didn't teach you to accept yourself, teach yourself now!

Accept Yourself

Don't be embarrassed about your weaknesses. **No one is perfect, and no one has to be!** If you have any problems with this statement, repeat it over and over until it sinks into the depths of your being.

It's true that we have room to improve — but with our own strengths and with our own personality.

If you go to a restaurant, you can select foods and drinks from a menu. If you are buying a sofa, you can choose the size, shape, design, fabric, and color. But with personality traits, we must learn to manage with what the Creator gave us. We must learn to accept our own limitations, utilize what we have, and build on our strengths — not destroy ourselves by attempting to build on the foundations of others. A person without a voice shouldn't try to be an opera star. Each of us has his unique array of character and personality traits, talents, and strong points. We must build on the base that we have and take it in directions that we truly like and enjoy.

Reb Zusha of Anipoli, the brother of Reb Elimelech of Lyzhensk, is reported to have said, "When I am brought to my final judgment, Hashem won't ask me why I wasn't like Moshe Rabbeinu, or Rabbi Akiva, or even like my holy brother Elimelech. He will ask me why I wasn't the best possible Zusha."

Only someone who builds on his own personal reality can succeed. Don't be afraid to be yourself. **The real you is infinitely better than an imitation of someone else.**

Take Control of Your Life

"Excuses for sale, ladies and gentleman!" cried a bent, ragged peddler. "Excuses, real cheap!"

"For twenty years you've been selling excuses," said the people in the marketplace, "and you're still poor!"

"That's how it is with excuses," the old peddler explained. "Even if people 'buy' your excuses, you'll never get rich from them."

It is said that success has many fathers, but failure is an orphan. We all know this from life experience. When individuals or organizations are successful, they take the credit. When they fail, they look around for someone or something to blame. Bad luck, an unhappy childhood, their parents or teachers, friends or *chavrusas*, the environment, society at large — any will do as a scapegoat.

You hear people saying, "If only I had the right connections," "If only I were married to the right person," "If only people understood me."

Excuses, excuses. Some better than others, but excuses nevertheless.

What's so harmful about excuses?

The Trap of Excuses

"If only" thoughts are immeasurably destructive. Reality cannot be changed. What these thoughts accomplish is to make a person miserable, sap his energy, and lead him to depression. What can come out of someone who sees himself as a lost suitcase that was sent to an airport in an unknown country?

Besides, focusing on what cannot be changed diverts attention and energy from what can be fixed.

It may very well be that people and circumstances have made our lives more difficult. But as long as we blame others for our problems, our chances of finding a solution are minuscule. "It's not my fault" means it isn't under my control; and if that's the case, there's nothing I can do about it but weep over my bitter fate — which won't get me anywhere. Imagine Sara saying that she won't eat at the conclusion of the Yom Kippur fast because "Rivka should have brought the cake and coffee!" Sara might even be right; but will that satisfy her hunger?

Unless we recognize that we ourselves are personally and exclusively responsible for our situation, we won't be able to improve it. Finding a solution for a problem that is someone else's fault is like losing keys in a dark alley and then searching for them under the lamppost because it's easier to see there.

Why, then, do we make excuses?

An excuse is a defense mechanism. We use it defend ourselves from others, but more often from ourselves. Deep down inside we know that we could do better, and we're filled with guilt feelings. If we can "prove" by means of excuses that it's not our fault, we can get off scot-free.

We never really get off scot-free, though. Our conscience doesn't rest. It will always rebuke us and reject our excuses, making us miserable — because any excuse can be refuted.

Any Excuse Can Be Refuted

A *poor man, a rich man, and a wicked man come before the heavenly court.*

They ask the poor man, "Why didn't you study Torah?" If he replies, "I was poor and busy trying to eke out a livelihood," they say, "Were you poorer than Hillel, who studied Torah in abject poverty?"

They ask the rich man, "Why didn't you study Torah?" If he replies, "I was rich and busy with my assets," they say, "Were you richer than R' Eliezer ben Charsom, who left the fortune he had inherited to go and study Torah?"

They ask the wicked man, "Why didn't you study Torah?" If he replies, "I was handsome and busy with my evil inclination," they say, "Were you handsomer than Joseph, who nevertheless resisted the advances of Potiphar's wife?" (Yoma 35b).

Although here our Sages mention only three common excuses that people use to justify their misguided paths, the message is that any excuse can be refuted. For any defect on which we try to blame our shortcomings in serving G-d, there is someone who had a much heavier dose of the same defect, yet was righteous.

Some say, "It's my nature; I can't change it." Nonsense. The type of "nature" that we can't change is the law of gravity and the weather. Our character traits *are* under our control. People are not born crooked, self-conscious, or fearful. True, we are born with certain tendencies. But we choose which of them to develop and strengthen. Any character trait is a habit that we have chosen to adopt — and that we can choose to break.

All winners throughout history, whether their achievements were in service of G-d or in other areas, took personal responsibility for their situation and took action to improve it. They did not look for scapegoats or wait for others to solve their problems for them.

Destitute orphans have made it to the top, and pampered children have dropped to the bottom; slow learners who persevered in their studies have became *roshei yeshivah,* and geniuses have learned nothing; peddlers have became millionaires, and heirs have lost fortunes.

J ohn Milton wrote Paradise Lost after he went blind, and Francisco Goya produced his most imaginative and powerful paintings after he lost his hearing.

❖   ❖   ❖

F rom the age of 12, Thomas Edison didn't hear a bird chirp, but he declared that his deafness was more of a blessing than a curse. It motivated him to read and allowed him total concentration, which paid off in terms of the 1,093 inventions that he patented.

❖   ❖   ❖

E leven years after he was crippled by polio, Franklin D. Roosevelt entered the White House in a wheelchair. He pulled the American economy out of the

Great Depression with his New Deal, led the United States through World War II, and became the only American president ever elected to four terms in office.

❖   ❖   ❖

*B*y 1819, the music in Ludwig van Beethoven's head was the only thing he could hear. In his diary he wrote, "Can anything prevent you from expressing your soul in music?" In 1824, he finished his Ninth Symphony, which concludes with the "Ode to Joy." Beethoven himself conducted the first performance. Only after a musician gently turned him to face the audience did he become aware of the wild applause of the crowd.

❖   ❖   ❖

*A*ndrew Carnegie was 13 when he came to the United States from Scotland and went to work in a cotton factory together with his father. Later he got a job as a railroad clerk, worked his way up, made some investments, and eventually became a steel manufacturer. The poor immigrant boy retired with half a billion dollars and devoted himself to philanthropy.

❖   ❖   ❖

*H*enry Morton Stanley grew up in a workhouse, where the headmaster beat the orphans cruelly, sometimes even to death. Nevertheless, he wanted to make a contribution to mankind. He became a journalist, found the long-lost Livingstone ("Dr.

Livingstone, I presume?") *and explored Africa with him, opening it to the world.*

No external circumstances or people absolutely determine our future, on either the material plane or the spiritual one.

Some of the great rebbes were handicapped, but did not let this stop them from leading their chassidim.

The Rebbe of Koznitz, author of Avodas Yisrael, had very weak legs; there were periods when he could not walk at all. R' Eizik'l of Kaliv suffered from a rare skin disease. He could not wear ordinary clothing, but only garments made of paper(!) (see Eser Kedushos). The charity of R' Chaim of Sanz, author of Divrei Chaim, was legendary; his lameness is less well known.

❖   ❖   ❖

In the late 19th century, a melamed came with his small family to America in search of a livelihood. He refused to compromise his Yiddishkeit and was unable to support his family, so he returned to Europe. But he left 13-year-old Yaakov Yosef behind; he had no money for his son's ticket.

The boy had a job working for a furrier for $1.25 a week, and he lived with relatives who charged him $1 a week. One Friday shortly after his parents' departure, the relatives raised the rent to $1.25.

Yaakov Yosef immediately left, bought himself three rolls, and slept that Shabbos on a park bench.

It might have been natural for him to harbor resentment against those relatives or his parents. But he took a different route. He resolved to work and save up money to bring his parents back, and to welcome the

homeless when he had his own home. He accom-
plished both objectives, while playing a key role in
building Yiddishkeit in America. R' Sholom Schwadron
called R' Yaakov Yosef Herman, hero of "All for the
Boss," "the Chafetz Chaim of America."

❖ ❖ ❖

*T**he cards were really stacked against Meir Feist
(1907–1975). On the physical side, he was paralyzed from the waist down in early childhood, and
his lungs could not expand normally, so he was constantly short of breath. On the spiritual side, he was
born in Mount Vernon, New York, and came to Torah
late in life.*

*He learned aleph-beis from the local rabbi and
began to study Gemara by himself at home with the
aid of a dictionary. Within a few years, he had covered all of Shas, acquiring broad knowledge and
deep understanding.*

*Reb Meir shopped, cooked, and cleaned for himself,
and he opened a store when he sold sheet music. But
he spent every free minute studying Torah. He became
well versed in Yoreh De'ah (and was ordained as a
rabbi) as well as mussar and chassidus, and implement-
ed whatever he learned. He said all prayers with utmost
care. He spoke in many yeshivos and synagogues, drew
people back to Judaism, and continued to encourage
them thereafter.*

*He loved people and treated everyone with friendli-
ness and respect. He was so grateful for their help and
so concerned about their problems that when a young
drug addict broke into his house, Reb Meir — alone
and helpless — persuaded him to give up the habit
and arranged for his rehabilitation.*

Reb Meir, who never married, rejoiced
fortune of others as if it were his own. Ye
would tell him of their engagements and
heartfelt blessings. His face shone wit
times. His Torah study, mitzvah obse..............
constant efforts at self-improvement kept him full of
zest. A book written about him was called The Face
That Shone.

Where there's a will, there's a way. Excuses are not arguments for what we cannot change, but for what we don't want to change. When someone says "I can't," what he really means is "I don't want to."

Drop the excuses and take charge of your life.

Open the Door

For twenty years, a prisoner sat isolated in a tower, sustained only by the food and drink that kindhearted people sent up by rope. He wept inconsolably over his bitter fate, mourning his lost freedom and lost opportunities.

Then, one day, he walked over to the door and turned the handle. To his astonishment, it wasn't locked. He was a free man! And he had been free all along. During all those years of misery, he had been a prisoner only of his imagination.

We are not so different from this prisoner. We look at the many obstacles strewn along the way to our goal and lament our inability to overcome them. We mourn the aspirations that we will never be able to attain because of our environment, family, and ability.

But in truth, the sky's the limit as to what we can reach. We can take off in any direction and to any height we wish — on condition that we don't sit with arms folded and blame others for installing locks that exist only in our imagination. If we are determined to succeed, if we jump into the turbulent sea of life firmly resolved to spare no effort to fulfill our mision, we will arrive safely at the shore of our goal. And we will find that all the obstacles were merely optical illusions.

Each person is the way he is for only one reason: He chose to be that way.

Even if he thinks the decision was forced on him, in reality it was not. If we really want to change and we invest the necessary effort, we *can* be different.

We do begin life with certain tendencies, but it is up to us to decide what to do with them. We ourselves choose which of our natural characteristics to develop and strengthen. We have the power to educate ourselves and to change our less-than-perfect characteristics for the better — if we *know* that we have this power. And we can learn how to take control of our lives if we invest effort, energy, and willpower.

We can and must put all our energy into doing what is correct for us. No one has the right or the power to interfere.

We alone shut the doors to success. We ourselves shut our eyes to the unlimited vista on the horizon. We ourselves shackle our hands and feet so that we can't take the steps needed to succeed. The barriers that hold us back are figments of our imagination.

If we overcome these imaginary impediments, we will be able to break out of our prison.

Repeat to yourself: "Nothing is blocking my way."

Develop Independence

Many people stop developing their independence at a certain stage because it frightens them. Instead of figuring out how to solve their own problems, they are more comfortable leaving it to others. If others don't push them to move in a certain way, they feel exempt from moving.

If you believe that you are dependent on others, then you are. The same goes for independence.

Dependent people put the emphasis on others. "*You* must help me. Whether I succeed or fail is in *your* hands."

Or: "It's *your* fault I failed; *you* have to get me out of ı mess." People who use this approach never see themselv as blameworthy. The trouble is always that *"they* aren't helping me."

Independent people put the emphasis on "I." They will say, *"I* must help myself. *I* am responsible for my own success. If *I* failed, *I* must find a way to get out of this mess."

Independence means not being afraid. Don't be afraid to take action yourself when you can, and don't be afraid to accept help when you can't.

If you want to actualize yourself, you must become independent. Be proactive: Act instead of reacting, initiate instead of being set in motion. Why hand over control of your life to others?

Take Responsibility

A storm broke out at sea, and the surging waves threatened to sink the ship. On board were two sailors. One sat around complaining: "If the ship were stronger, this wouldn't be happening!" The other had no time to complain. He was busy trying everything he could think of to save the ship.

In life's stormy sea, there is only way to save your ship from sinking: Take control of yourself!

G-d created good and evil, He gave us the power to choose between them, and He commanded us to choose the good. This would not be possible if our behavior were the inevitable product of circumstances. You and I are responsible for the way our lives go.

Responsibility doesn't mean that what happens is my fault; it means that the choice of what to do and the power to decide to change are in my hands. Responsibility means that I am going to determine what happens through a decision that I am going to make.

Recognize your right to choose freely. As long as you don't have the guts to say frankly, "I chose to do this," you won't be able to say, "Today I choose to do differently." As long as you claim that you were forced to live the way you do, you will have to wait until you are forced to change direction. Only after you recognize that *you* chose to be as you are will you be able to change.

Would we think of entering a car whose driver lets go of the steering wheel? But how do *we* drive through life? Do we grasp the wheel firmly? Do we slow down, stop, and change direction as necessary?

True, it's scary to take responsibility for our own life. If we stop blaming others for our shortcomings, we will have to change. And changing means facing the unknown, which is like the haunted house in an amusement park — you don't know what will pop out at you next, and whether you will be able to cope. Fear of the unknown prevents some people from seeing a psychologist; they would rather continue suffering than try something new.

We must overcome our fear of change. Only when we learn to take control into our own hands will we be able to move forward toward our goal.

It's your life. Take responsibility for it.

Tell the truth! Say "I want to" or "I have decided to" instead of "I have to." Say "I'm afraid to" or "I refuse to" instead of "I can't."

If ever you catch yourself saying, "If only things were different, I would" — stop yourself right there.

Things are *not* different, and you can't change the world. You have to accept reality and live with it. But that doesn't mean you should go through life feeling helpless and losing everything you want to — and can — achieve. In every situation you can't control, there's always some part that you can. You can't control the weather, but you can shield yourself against it with a coat, umbrella, radiator, or air-conditioner. If you are stuck in heavy traffic, you can do isometric exercises, listen to tapes, or plan the next day's schedule.

If you lost your way, would it help to sit and complain about the lack of road signs? If you slipped and fell, would it help to lie there and complain about the banana peel that was left on the sidewalk?

If you've gotten lost in life, go out and search for the road to happiness. If you have fallen, stand up on your feet; don't wait for others to pick you up!

> *Lech lecha me'artzecha, "Go from your earthliness" (Bereishis 12:1–3). Some Jews blame their character flaws on the pull of the material world; others, on their birth; still others, on their teachers. To all of them, G-d says: "Go from your earthliness, from your relatives, and from your father's house" — stop the excuses. If you sincerely want to improve your ways from here on in, I will show you the right path; go "to the land that I will show you." Are you afraid that you lack the wisdom for it? "I will make of you a great nation" — I will give you a lofty soul that will help you. Then you will rise so high that "you shall be a blessing" — you will have the power to bless others. Moreover, "all the families of the earth shall bless themselves by you" — the whole world will point to you and say, "He's on the right track. Follow him!" (R' Chaim of Sanz, Pri Tzaddik 7).*

Develop
Your Potential

hree brothers inherited equally large sums from their father. One invested the money carefully and tripled his capital. Another invested rashly and lost it all. The third stored his inheritance in a vault. It remained as he had received it, except for losing some of its value through inflation.

We are all born with special, unique talents that our heavenly Father gave us — in potential. To succeed in life, we have to develop these talents and learn new skills. That takes tremendous effort, energy, and willpower. But people invest everything they have in beautiful homes, impressive clothes, and other temporal things. Isn't it much more important to invest in improving our personal abilities in order to realize our potential?

The difference between those who influence, change, and move people and things (the "movers and shakers") and those who don't is that the ones who do, have faith in their own ability to acquire more know-how.

Never stand still! No matter what your current situation in life, always try to climb up another step, and yet another. It doesn't matter whether your ladder is based on a mountain or in a valley. As long as you go up another step, you will be higher than you were before.

Don't let your life become static, fixed, and routine. Stagnant water becomes putrid, but a flowing river is a source of delight. Plan your life so that it is full of excitement and challenge, so that each day is different from the other. Of the mitzvos G-d says, "that I command you today" (*Devarim* 6:6) — they should be fresh to you as if they were given today (*Rashi*). Let's open new horizons, learn new things, and occasionally do something different, so that our lives will be interesting and full of satisfaction. Not only will we blossom and grow, enjoying every moment, but, in addition, people will enjoy being in our company.

We can and must make the most of ourselves.

Use Your Brain

It takes brainpower to succeed in any realm, especially in serving G-d. "It is impossible to be properly G-d-fearing unless you are wise," wrote the *Ibn Ezra* (on *Shemos* 18:21). Wisdom is essential for the perfection of man: "He who has this (wisdom) within him has everything within him. He who does not have this within him what is within him? If he has acquired this, what does he lack? If he has not acquired this, what has he acquired?" (*Nedarim* 41a). Just as G-d created the world through wisdom, so must a person create a new nature for himself through his wisdom (*Degel Machaneh Efrayim, Bereishis*).

"What can I do if G-d didn't make me smart?" asks Zev in frustration. He quotes the Gemara: "The angel in charge of conception takes the drop before G-d and asks, 'Master of the world, what will this drop be? Mighty or weak? Wise or foolish? Rich or poor?' " (*Niddah* 16b). Zev continues, "When the angel did that with me, it was decreed that I would be stupid."

But the *Rambam* disagrees:

> Do not think that G-d decrees upon a person from the beginning of his creation to be righteous or wicked. It is not so. Every single person can become as righteous as Moshe or as wicked as Yeravam, wise or foolish, merciful or cruel, stingy or generous. No one forces him, decrees concerning him, or draws him to one of the two paths. He himself knowingly bends to whichever path he wishes. As Yirmiyahu said, "Evil and good do not emanate from the mouth of the Most High" (*Eichah* 3:38) — the Creator does not decree that a person will be good or bad (*Hilchos Teshuvah* 5:2).

Actually there is no contradiction between the *Rambam* and the Gemara. Torah study simply makes the foolish wise. It increases intelligence (*Chovos HaLevavos, Shaar Avodas HaElokim*, Ch. 2). The Mishnah says: "Anyone whose fear of sin precedes his wisdom, his wisdom will endure" (*Avos* 3:11) — for if he fears sin, then even if it was decreed upon him to be foolish, he will turn wise!

On the other hand, someone who does not study Torah is liable to lose his natural wisdom.

Intelligence is not so much what we have received as what we do with what we have received.

*F*ifteen-year-old Velvel was astonished when a close friend in yeshivah leaped ahead of him. After a few weak attempts to catch up, Velvel told me he was finished. He watched in anguish as the gap *between the two boys increased — a gap that he saw no way of bridging.*

This is a mistake. It is true that G-d granted each of us a certain measure of intelligence, but He also gave us the choice to develop what we have or neglect it until it rusts. Each of us has the ability to develop his mind and sharpen his thinking.

Children who were not bright have grown up to be brilliant Torah scholars.

aharam Shik, one of the great disciples of the Chasam Sofer, once said that he was born with a "pumpkin head." He could not absorb the Gemara, and sometimes had to review his studies forty times before it sank in. Through toil and prayer, he merited to become wise (Darchei Moshe HeChadash 6; R' Shaul Brach).

❖   ❖   ❖

R' Yaakov of Lissa (the Nesivos), author of Chavas Daas and Nesivos HaMishpat, was not bright as a child.

❖   ❖   ❖

n his volume of halachic responsa, R' Yitzchak of Pozna wrote that as a youngster, he had a "weak head" and didn't understand his studies; only through prayer did he become great (Introduction, She'elos U'Teshuvos, R' Yitzchak MiPozna).

❖   ❖   ❖

R' Yitzchak Elchanan Spector (author of Kovetz Shiurim) was not born with special aptitude. Diligence turned him into one of the great halachic authorities of his time.

❖   ❖   ❖

It is well known that the contemporary gaon, R' Chaim Kanievsky of Bnei Brak, had difficulty studying Gemara as a child.

Before we have strained ourselves to the maximum of human ability and used every bit of the brainpower that we do have, how can we complain about not having more?

If you covered one healthy eye with a bandage, could you complain about having only one useful eye? If you had a lot of money in the bank but didn't bother withdrawing it, could you complain about living in poverty? If you don't work at sharpening your mind and utilizing your potential, how can you complain that G-d didn't give you enough intelligence?

Cultivate Your Field

G-d endowed each field with a natural potential for yielding crops, but unless it is cultivated, it will yield weeds. He endowed each person with a certain measure of wisdom, but we must work on ourselves to bring out our potential.

R' Moshe Chaim Luzzatto, author of Mesillas Yesharim, wrote:

Observation shows that G-d gave man a large share in developing and completing this world. We can even say that the original Creation was only a starting point and a potential; its completion was left in the hands of man. Thus our Sages said that everything from the orig-

inal Creation requires fixing: wheat must be ground, lupines must be sweetened, and so on.

Turnus Rufus asked R' Akiva, "Which deeds are better, those of heaven or those of man?"

R' Akiva replied, "Those of man."

To prove it, R' Akiva brought sheaves and pastries and asked him, "Which is better?"

Natural things left wild do not work perfectly until man cultivates them. The fruit of an uncultivated wild tree does not compare in taste or beauty to the fruit of a cultivated one. The earth itself, if not fertilized and tilled, will not give forth its produce at all.

The Creator left opportunities for people to show their abilities by improving on nature.

The same applies to the mind of man himself. If intelligence is planted in him to begin with, and he doesn't develop it, he will be like the uncultivated tree or the neglected soil. The tree still yields fruit and he will still learn many things, but the fruits of a cultivated tree or of developed intelligence are incomparably improved. Just as a person needs training in various subjects in order to realize the potential of his intelligence, so does he need to train his mind itself, so that his thinking will be clear and orderly (Sefer HaHigayon, Introduction).

Although each of us came into this world with a certain portion of intelligence, we have the power to cultivate it so that it yields beautiful fruit.

Learn One New Thing Each Day

How can intelligence be improved? Various methods have been given (see, for instance, *Akeidas Yitzchak* on *Va'eschanan*). There's one that I find particularly easy and effective.

I once read about a clever man who resolved not to go to sleep at night until he had learned one new thing that day.

I've seen such resolutions produce dramatic personal changes for many people. Working to acquire wisdom daily not only expands your knowledge but also increases your general motivation.

Mr. Hollander complained that he was bored with life. "If I were to give you a sleeping pill that would put you to sleep for three months straight," I said, "would you take it?"

"What a question!" he answered, with an embarrassed smile. "I wish I could turn the clock ahead and become a few years older."

"If you earned a few thousand dollars each week," I continued, "would you still agree to do it?"

Without hesitation: "Certainly not."

Evidently, Mr. Hollander felt he was not acquiring anything significant in life. Such people move through this world like caged animals. Is it any wonder they don't feel the joy of being alive?

I was once working with disgruntled teenagers. Since they lacked the desire to study, they said, they were doing nothing in school and "going out of their minds from boredom."

No wonder they felt that way. How could they *not* be bored if they were doing nothing?

Banking on the theory that everyone wants to know more, I said, "Isn't it a shame to live such a life? There are so many fascinating things in the world: the miracles of nature, the wonders of technology, the curiosities of history, the workings of the mind, and so many other subjects that you can study to expand your horizons."

After I had piqued their intellectual curiosity, I challenged them to acquire one new piece of knowledge each day, in any field they wanted. The challenge was so easy and interesting that they willingly agreed.

They began to amass knowledge. I kept track of their progress. Every week, I would ask, "Have you become wiser this week?" In due time, I went a step further and suggested, "Let's sum up this week's acquisitions." Together we calculated how many minutes of acquiring wisdom they had put in during the past seven days. When they saw how little effort they had invested, they began to put in more time and achieve more and more. In the process of working on themselves, they naturally improved in many important areas.

Believe it or not, many of these near-dropouts even began to study Torah diligently.

How did *that* happen?

By the prime-the-pump principle: Find one area that interests the person and start him working on it. Once he gets going, you can guide him into other areas as well.

"**T**he only thing that interests me," said Ben, "is business, and they don't teach that in yeshivah. So there's nothing for me to do there except get into trouble with the principal for cutting classes — especially Gemara."

"Okay," I said, "if you want to be a businessman, let me help you develop the qualities you'll need to be a good one. Just make me a list, and we'll work on them together."

A few days later, Ben came to me with his list:

In order to succeed in business, you must have self-control and self-confidence. You need to be able to:

- deal with all types of characters, including nudniks
- negotiate shrewdly
- keep cool under stress
- make decisions without hesitating
- take calculated risks

Ben was well aware that he didn't possess the qualities on his list, and he agreed enthusiastically to work toward acquiring them. We drew up a plan of action and a schedule of study. He began with a book about getting along with people and another on basic business math.

Adopting a study regimen helped Ben acquire self-discipline. When he saw how much knowledge he was acquiring, he decided to add a few halachos to his daily "preparation for business" study schedule.

By the time three months had passed, Ben was attending all classes regularly, and by the end of the year, he had even taken extracurricular tests on large portions of Gemara.

Time and again I have seen that by arousing a person's natural curiosity and his thirst for wisdom and self-improvement, it's easy enough to steer him toward the right path.

Give someone a finger of interest, and he'll want the whole hand. Present him with a challenge to gain a little wisdom, and he'll aspire to much.

Try it out on yourself, and see how much truth there is in it. **Resolve not to go to sleep at night until you have acquired one new piece of wisdom.** This is a sure way to increase your motivation and enthusiasm.

Enthusiasm

The fuel that drives winners to the finish line is joy and enthusiasm. If you don't believe me, check among your friends and acquaintances, and see whether you can find a single winner who is bored with his field of endeavor.

Where does enthusiasm come from? I claim that it starts with a feeling of lack.

In order to *do* anything, you must first *want* something. And in order to *want* something, you must first feel that you *lack* it. Taking action because you want to fill a lack is what makes us enthusiastic about doing. The more passionately you want something, and the more you expect to enjoy it, the more enthusiastically you will work for it. The hard work and joyous creativity will both fill you with zest and boost your chances of success.

If joy is missing in someone's life, it's because he is not working to fill his lack. He discharges his duties without desire and will — and the results are dismal.

Who determines what your lack is? Only you.

C hanoch is poor. He lives with his wife and five children in a small, rundown apartment. In my opinion, he lacks money. In his opinion, he lacks spirituality. He is content with his financial situation and isn't interested in working to improve it. His hunger is for more Torah knowledge. Early in the morning and late at night, weekdays and weekends, he pores over sefarim without letup.

Before I discovered the secret of lack, I would often wonder why the rich don't stop working. If I had a lot of money, I would put it all in the bank, live off the interest, and enjoy life. Why do they keep on working hard?

The answer is that if they didn't feel a hunger for more, they wouldn't have gotten where they are. The hunger is in their blood, and it pushes them to keep working without letup.

To the question "Who is rich?" our Sages did not answer "He who makes do with his lot" but "He who is *happy* with his lot" (*Avos* 4:1). If someone becomes complacent and stops aspiring to more, that's the beginning of the end. Such a person exists but is not alive.

Someone once asked at a funeral, "How old was he when he died?" A clever person replied, "He died when he was 30. Now they're burying him at the age of 65."

The feeling of lack is what has been prodding us to learn, develop, and progress since we were infants. A toddler whose parents always understand and act on his nonverbal communications won't feel the need to speak or act, and consequently he won't learn to do so. A child begins to study Torah only after his teachers have set him a challenge — perhaps in the form of a question or a prize — that stimulates the desire and will to learn. No one reacts without stimulus, external or internal.

If we lack motivation, it is probably because we aren't attuned to our true inner needs, and therefore we aren't excited about anything. There are no shortcuts. We must examine ourselves to discover what we truly want.

Laziness?

We usually call someone who doesn't do anything with himself "lazy."

He isn't.

Normal people aren't lazy; they're simply not interested. The things they are expected to do don't satisfy them, so naturally they lack the will and desire to do them. Every "lazy" person will work furiously to pursue what truly interests him. "Alacrity is the result of inner enthusiasm" (*Mesillas Yesharim,* Ch. 7).

> *A yeshivah student told me that he was lazy by nature and asked me to help him overcome this nature. "I try to study," said Yitzchak, "but it just doesn't go."*
>
> *"Were you ever late for an outing with your friends?" I asked.*
>
> *"No."*
>
> *"If they gave out $1,000 to whoever crossed an intersection that was a 15-minute walk away from here, would you go?"*
>
> *Yitzchak's eyes lit up. "I would run!"*
>
> *"If so, you're not lazy," I told him. "Studying simply doesn't interest you. You have other ideas in your head and you aspire to other things."*

Indeed, in the course of our sessions I discovered a youth whose interests lay elsewhere. When I got him working on areas in which he was interested, he proved to be a diligent fellow.

Choose your words carefully. If you are trying to help someone improve, do not tell him he is lazy. Not only is it inaccurate, it also makes him feel that he cannot change, because that is his nature. Tell him the truth: Point out that he is not interested in doing what is being demanded of him. Help him discover what really interests him. If you want to guide him "on the right path," help him become aware that he will be lacking something if he does not go that route; in this way, you can arouse in him the will and desire to do and to work on himself.

Just a minute. Why speak about others? Don't we ourselves suffer from "laziness"?

In the Spiritual Realm

*L*evi and R' Shimon were learning with R' Yehudah HaNasi. After they finished one Book of Scripture, R' Yehudah asked what they wanted to study next. Levi chose Mishlei, but R' Shimon preferred Tehillim. R' Shimon prevailed, and they began to study Tehillim. When they reached the verse "His desire is in the Torah of Hashem" (Tehillim 1:2), R' Yehudah explained, "A person can learn Torah only from the area that his heart desires." Levi then said, "My master, you have hereby granted me permission to rise and retire" (Avodah Zarah 19a). Not only didn't R' Yehudah rebuke Levi for not wanting to study Tehillim, he actually permitted him to stop learning it.*

So what if Levi had no desire for it? Let's take a look at Rashi's comment on "A person can learn Torah only from the area that his heart desires": His teacher should teach him only a tractate that he requests. For if he teaches him a different tractate, it will not endure, since his heart is on his desire.

The student's heart is "on his desire," that is, on what he *wants* to know. Unless he feels that he lacks that tractate, he won't have the will to learn it — and without that will, he won't succeed!

To succeed in any field, you must forge ahead with gusto and enthusiasm and invest all your energy in what you are doing. This includes the spiritual realm.

Of course we all must keep the 613 mitzvos regardless of whether we find them enjoyable and fulfilling. But to keep a mitzvah perfectly, we must do it with joyous enthusiasm, not in a dull, routine way. "Every day they should be as new in your eyes" (*Rashi, Devarim* 26:16) — it's natural to be enthusiastic about something new, and we need to be enthusiastic about serving G-d. The highest level is "to serve Hashem with gladness" (*Tehillim* 100:2).

> Every single mitzvah that comes a person's way is a gift sent to him by the Holy One, Blessed is He, and his reward will increase in accordance with his joy.
>
> Thus the Arizal revealed that all that he acquired — the opening of the gates of wisdom and Divine inspiration to him — was in reward for his doing each mitzvah with immeasurable joy. He said: This is what is meant by the verse: "Because you have not served Hashem, your G-d, with gladness and with a merry heart merov kol" (Devarim 28:47). Merov kol means "more than an abundance of everything" — more than you enjoy worldly pleasures, gold, gems, and pearls (Sefer Chareidim, Tena'im LeKiyum HaMitzvos).

How can we acquire the will to serve G-d? By studying books of *mussar* and *chassidus* that arouse an awareness of what is lacking in our service, for this stimulates will and desire for improvement. Then we will feel creative joy in serving G-d, and we will find fulfillment in our achievements.

The Four P's

"I believe in luck," said Sam Shoen, founder of U-Haul. "The harder I work, the luckier I get."

No one succeeds in any field without investing mighty efforts born of inner conviction in the correctness of his way and his ability to win. The only thing someone can do well without any effort is to slip on a banana peel.

Of course, everyone must relax a bit from time to time to renew his strength. But don't waste your life resting. Imagine someone who has embarked on a long, hard journey by foot. In the middle, he says to himself, "It's so hard!" He finds himself a grassy spot at the side of the road and decides to stay there, basking in the warm sunshine. He may be able to stay there a long time and even to enjoy it, but he'll never arrive at his destination.

Researchers who wanted to learn how success is achieved distributed questionnaires to large groups of people and followed up many years later. They discovered that the ones who succeeded were not those with special talents or resources, but *those who persisted stubbornly* until they reached their goal. Check what became of your old classmates, and you'll find the same results.

Talent is helpful, but it doesn't guarantee success. Thomas Edison defined genius as "one percent inspiration, 99 percent perspiration." What guarantees success is the four P's — Perspiration, Persistence, Patience, and Paying the price.

Beethoven's notebooks show that he worked with great care, often for many years, tirelessly revising the themes and their implementation until he produced his masterpieces.

Thomas Edison spent two years looking for a filament that would light up without burning up. He tried 700 different items, from the red hair of a boy whose life he had saved to a piece of sewing thread that he baked. The baked thread worked; the first lightbulb glowed for two days.

Never stop moving forward. If you fall, pick yourself up and keep on going, keep on trying. Eventually, you'll reach your goal.

Perhaps that is what our Sages meant when they said: "One who learns a chapter 100 times cannot be compared to one who learns it 101 times" (*Chagigah* 9b). Sometimes the difference between success and failure lies in one extra try.

Patience

On Monday, Richard purchased a successful chain of stores. Early Tuesday morning, he instructed his managers to open them at 9 — and then close them all at 9:10 to assess his earnings. Not surprisingly, the assessment "showed" that he had gone bankrupt.

If a farmer sows fruitful land with high-quality seeds, and goes out to the field two days later to see the crop, he will be bitterly disappointed. Farmers need to plow, sow, and water their fields, and then wait very, very patiently for the seeds to sprout.

Child-rearing is like farming. You can't force your child to be the way you want him to be. You can only plant seeds in his heart, water them with love and discipline, and wait very, very patiently for them to sprout. Chances are good that fifteen years from now, your 3-year-old daughter will no longer suck her thumb, the fighting between your 9- and 10-year-old sons will have evolved into close friendship, and your teenage rebel will be settled into refined adulthood.

Whether you are starting a business, giving up cigarettes, or preventing a divorce, the process takes time. It has to run its course, with plenty of ups and downs along the way. You can't rush it.

Demanding instant results is the surest way to sabotage any project. Countless people have thrown in the towel only because they didn't have the patience necessary to persevere until they were successful.

Do Not Evaluate Results Prematurely

Those who don't learn this secret break early in the game. I've seen yeshivah students start off on the right foot and work on themselves methodically, only to give up in despair when they didn't reach their lofty goals overnight.

> **"I** have to struggle to do what's right," Menashe told me sadly, "If only I were the way you're supposed to be, I wouldn't have such temptations. It proves that I have an unusually coarse soul."

To a youth like Menashe, R' Yitzchak Hutner wrote:

> It is terrible that when we learn about the spiritual giants of our people, we learn only about the final

summary of their greatness. We speak of their perfection but skip their raging internal struggles. The impression we get is that they were born with their stature and character. Everyone puts the Chafetz Chaim's purity of speech up on a pedestal — but one in a thousand knows about all the struggles and setbacks he went through in the course of his war with his evil inclination.

The result is that when a youth who has spirit and ambition finds himself experiencing obstacles and declines, he thinks he is not "planted in the house of G-d." For in his imagination, that means sitting tranquilly on green fields by peaceful waters, enjoying his good inclination like the righteous enjoy the radiance of the Divine Presence in the Garden of Eden; it means not being agitated by the storm of the evil inclination — like the dead, who are free of it at last.

The wisest of men said, "Seven shall the righteous one fall, and rise" (Mishlei 24:16). This does not mean that even if the righteous one falls seven times, he will still rise. Rather, the righteous one rises through his seven falls!

"G-d saw all that He had made, and behold it was very good" (Bereishis 1:31) — "good" is the good inclination; "very," the evil one (Bereishis Rabbah 9:7). My dear friend, I embrace you to my heart and whisper in your ear, that if your letter had told me about your mitzvos and good deeds, I would have called it a good letter. But since it speaks of struggles and setbacks, I call it a very good letter.

Your spirit is agitated with your ambition to achieve greatness. Please do not picture our spiritual giants as being identical with their good inclinations. Rather, picture them waging a terrible war against their own base tendencies. And when you *feel the storm of the evil inclination raging inside you, know that in this you resemble them much more than when you are in the state of tranquillity you so desire. Ultimately, the area in which you have the most trouble is precisely the one in which you are going to reveal the glory of Heaven the most! (Igaros U'Michtavim, Iggeres 128).*

These words should be engraved on the portals of each yeshivah. How many have been devastated by this inevitable complication of human nature! How many could have reached astounding successes had they known this secret!

When Helping Others

Many fine educators and counselors fail only because they give up too quickly.

People with problems lack faith in their ability to solve them. As a result, they approach the work of self-improvement with reservations — and the results show it. Many don't need advice so much as encouragement and motivation, which takes time. You have to instill in them belief that they *can* solve their problems even if they don't see immediate improvement. This belief will empower them to do what they need to do.

If you persist patiently, you are much likelier to succeed.

Marvin's behavior had gotten out of control. Hardly a day went by without a fistfight.

I worked with him for a few weeks, but we made no headway. "The whole project is a waste of time," he would say. "You think you're the first one to try? No one has been able to help me yet — and you can't, either!"

Experience had taught me how hard it is to change, so I didn't give up. I kept encouraging Marvin to con-

*tinue working at it, even when it was very frustrating.
I gave him extra attention and placed more trust in him
than he or his parents did. I worked hard to make my
confidence in his eventual success rub off on him. My
enthusiasm was contagious, and eventually he began
to believe in himself.*

*That was when the turning point came. Lo and
behold, with help from Above and with joint efforts,
things started to move. Little by little, his heart opened
up, and the efforts I had put in began to bear fruit.*

Over the course of my career I have encountered many
Marvins.

Pay the Price

Everything in life has a price tag, commensurate with its
value. You can't attain impressive achievements without
investment any more than you can buy a six-room house for
the price of one door. Small efforts bring small successes; bigger efforts are needed for bigger success. What you put in is
what you get out.

Success comes with various price tags, from belt-
tightening and self-control to putting up with difficult people
and situations.

*When the Brooklyn Dodgers' general manager
decided to desegregate baseball, he asked
Jackie Robinson to join his league, but on one condition: that no matter what was said or done to him,
the black player wouldn't fight back. Although it
went against his nature, Robinson decided to pay
the price.*

*At first the fans booed, the sports writers said
Robinson played badly, and his teammates didn't talk
to him. Robinson never fought back.*

Within a few years, other black players were in the major leagues, and Robinson himself led the Brooklyn Dodgers to eight World Series and one championship.

Anyone can attain almost anything he wants — provided he is willing to pay the price, and to keep working patiently until he reaches his goal.

"Wait a minute," I can hear some readers saying. "This sounds like heresy! What happened to faith in G-d?"

You have every right to ask. I'll answer your question in the next chapter.

Have Faith in G-d

When the Stern Company went bankrupt, Mr. Stern became depressed. He stopped functioning almost totally and became apathetic toward his family and his surroundings. Often he would weep over his lot.

I tried to get him to think about what he could still do to improve the situation.

"Everything is in Hashem's hands," he said sadly. "And if this is His will, what's the use of trying?"

Then he looked at me in surprise. "Say, don't you have bitachon?"

When someone is tired of fighting an uphill battle, it's understandable for his spirits to sag. However, to lose hope and interest in life until a frightening fog of despair settles over him is another matter. And to drag a new partner into his unsuccessful affairs — no less than the Creator Himself?

Truth be told, all of us at times make this destructive mistake. When we succeed, our heart swells with pride. We take all the credit for ourselves. We attribute our success to *our* brains and *our* talents: "My strength and the might of my hand made me all this wealth!" (*Devarim* 8:17). When we fail, we crane our necks looking around for additional partners — parents, teachers, or friends —with whom we can share our failures. If we don't find anyone else, we remember the Creator. We lift our eyes heavenward and piously attribute our failures to Him. For yes, everyone is at fault — except we ourselves. *We* did not err. *We* are okay. But what can we do if G-d so decreed?

King Solomon put it this way: "A man's foolishness corrupts his way, and his heart rages against Hashem" (*Mishlei* 19:3). *Rashi* explains: When a person is foolish and sins, he is punished for it — whereupon he gets angry at G-d and complains about Divine justice.

Some people don't actualize their potential because they aren't willing to put in the effort. Others, acting on a momentary impulse rather than balanced judgment, make a mistake that wipes out everything they've built up in the course of years. Yet all of them say, "What did Hashem do?"

Moshe didn't manage to find a job. His friends tried to help, but without success. "What can I do if Hashem doesn't want me to succeed?" says Moshe. But what really happened is that he did not show up for appointments on time, so would-be employers concluded that he was unreliable.

❖　　　❖　　　❖

Yaakov's wife complains constantly about whatever he does or doesn't do. "Heaven decreed that I would have a bad wife," says Yaakov. The truth, *though, is that he doesn't keep his commitments or fulfill his minimum obligations to his family.*

No, G-d is not "guilty" of failures that stem from our lack of will to succeed. Our Father in Heaven is merciful and compassionate. He does not want what is bad for us; He does not want heartbreak for us. He gave us free choice and commanded us to choose life.

It is true that we must accept Divine judgment. We do recite the blessing *Baruch Dayan Emes,* "Blessed is the true Judge," upon hearing bad news. What, then, distinguishes sincere acceptance of Divine judgment from the use of "faith" as an excuse for blaming G-d?

Genuine faith and trust in G-d — awareness that there is a benevolent Creator watching over us — gladdens the heart and strengthens the spirit. If you operate out of an inner conviction that everything is in G-d's hands, you will see the light at the end of the tunnel. You will never fall into despair; you will never lose hope; you will never give up!

When someone bemoans his fate hopelessly, it is clear that he lacks the requisite trust. Gloom and frustration are signs that his "faith" is an escape from taking necessary action. He has stopped believing in himself and is afraid of trying and failing again. Paralyzing fear and timidity have taken control of him under the mask of faith.

If we turn into great believers only to soothe our consciences, which nag at us for our inaction, our "faith" is a fig leaf to cover our own weakness. If we feel hidden anger when we speak of His Providence, our "faith" is a mask to cover the lack of self-confidence that deters us from daring to try again.

We must do precisely the opposite. When we succeed, let us praise and thank G-d for the talents and abilities He has given us; let us be grateful to our parents and teachers, who invested so much effort in us; let us thank our friends and neighbors who encouraged and supported us when we needed it most. And when we fail — let us blame ourselves alone! Of course we must pray to G-d to help us, but together with this, we have an obligation to figure out where we have gone wrong, why the means we used did not yield the desired results, and what we can do to improve our situation.

To ascribe poor results of our efforts to heavenly decrees while we sit with arms folded is just as foolish as to boast that our talents brought us success.

"Do you mean to say that we decide our own fate?" you ask. "If so, where is faith?"

The Obligation to Try

Of course we must believe that a man does not stub his toe on earth if it was not so decreed in heaven (see *Chullin* 7b), and that without G-d's help, no one would be able to lift a finger, let alone take one step forward. We must also believe that if it was decreed that we will not succeed in a certain area, all the efforts in the world will not help us, and if it is decreed that we will acquire something, it will come our way even if we do nothing to get it. But we must remember that G-d created the world to operate in natural ways. And for the most part, even after it has been decreed that a person will attain something, he is still required to make the effort to get it.

How do we know that Divine blessing rests only on those who make this effort? The Torah says, "For Hashem will have blessed you in all your crop and *in all your handiwork*" (*Devarim* 15:10), and "In order that Hashem, your G-d, will bless you *in all your handiwork that you may undertake*" (ibid. 14:29). He will not bless you if you sit idle (*Sifri, Devarim* 123; *Midrash Tehillim* 136).

Chovos HaLevavos writes that unless G-d so wills, no man has the power to help or harm either himself or others, to increase or decrease his portion, or to hasten or postpone what befalls him; nevertheless, G-d's wisdom decreed that we must make an effort to acquire our needs. We see this with our own eyes. G-d may have sent Reuven bread, and it may be sitting on his table — but unless Reuven extends his hand to take the food and put it into his mouth, he will die of hunger! And if he has not bread but wheat, he must grind, knead, and bake it. If the wheat is still in the store, he must first buy it. If he doesn't have money to buy it, he must work or sell something to acquire the money (*Shaar HaBitachon*, Ch. 3).

Striving to acquire our needs does *not* contradict our belief that we cannot succeed unless G-d has so decreed.

Why does G-d want us to work to attain what He has decreed for us to have in any case?

One of the many answers is given by *Mesillas Yesharim* (Ch. 21):

> A person could have sat idle and the decree would have been fulfilled, were it not that all people are subject to the punishment of "By the sweat of your brow shall you eat bread" (Bereishis 3:19). Because of this, every person must make some effort for the sake of his livelihood, for so has the Supreme King decreed. It is like a tax that the whole human race must pay; there is no escaping it.

The Patriarch Yaakov got ready for a dangerous encounter with Esav in three ways: with prayers to G-d, tributes to Esav, and preparations for fight or flight (*Rashi, Bereishis* 32:9).

> This portion was written to make known that the Holy One, Blessed is He, saved His servant … and to teach us that Yaakov tried with all his might to save [himself and his family]. Furthermore, there is a hint here for

succeeding generations that whatever happened to our forefather with his brother Esav will happen to us always with Esav's children [the Western world], and we ought to follow the method of the righteous Yaakov and prepare ourselves in the three ways that he prepared himself: prayer, bribery, and preparations for escape (Ramban, Bereishis 32:4).

A person who sits back and imagines that he is thereby fulfilling the mitzvah of trusting in G-d is liable to put himself in danger. *Sefer HaChinuch* (546) discusses this point in connection with the mitzvah of making a fence around one's roof.

Although G-d supervises people in detail and knows their deeds, and although everything that will befall them, good or bad, is through His decree and command ... nevertheless we must guard ourselves against mishaps that occur in the world. For the Creator built His world on the foundations of Nature. He decreed that fire burns and water extinguishes the flames ... that if a large stone falls on a man's head, it will smash his skull, and that if a man falls off a roof that is high above the ground, he will die.

G-d graciously blew into our bodies an intelligent living soul to guard the body from all harm, and placed both of them, the soul and its body, into the natural world. And since G-d made man's body subservient to nature because it is physical, He commanded him to watch out lest nature, which is in His hands, hurt him.

Our Sages said: "One should not stand in a dangerous place and rely on a miracle, for perhaps a miracle will not be performed for him" (Shabbos 32a).

Similarly, you see throughout Scripture that even when the people of Israel went out to war at G-d's command, they waged their war and armed themselves as if they were relying solely on natural means. And so it is proper to do.

When a deadly epidemic breaks out in a city, people begin to question whether they should flee or not. Besides the practical implications, this matter also poses a philosophical dilemma: If it has been decreed for a person to die, how will fleeing help? If it has been decreed that he live, why should he leave? Indeed, it is virtually certain that some of those who remain will survive the epidemic, and, conversely, some of those who flee will die.

Mabit (*Beis Elokim, Shaar HaTefillah* 16) explains the following basic principle:

We all know that G-d determines on Rosh Hashanah who will live and who will die.

The people who remain in the city and survive the epidemic were judged, based on their actions, to absolutely be "inscribed in the book of life," while those who escape the town but die anyway had been condemned by their actions to absolutely be "inscribed in the book of death."

However, among those who were in the city when the epidemic began were others, whose actions the previous year did not result in so absolute a verdict. Some were people who, though their deeds warrant that they die, can have their sentence commuted by their going into exile. Also among those in the city are some who deserve to live, but who are not worthy of being miraculously spared from the epidemic.

The fate of the people in these categories will be determined by their own actions. A person in the first of these groups who escapes the city will live, for he has now undergone the requisite exile. On the other hand, a person in the latter group who remains in the city will die, for his merits are inadequate to spare him from the epidemic.

Since G-d knows on Rosh Hashanah what the person will ultimately choose to do, he judges the person accordingly, and establishes on Rosh Hashanah what the person's fate will be.

In spiritual accomplishments and in every aspect of serving G-d, the choice is definitely in our hands: "Everything is in the hands of heaven except for fear of Heaven" (*Berachos* 33b). In worldly matters, if He decreed that we will be poor, then even if we receive a chest filled with gold, it will slip through our fingers; and if He decreed that we will succeed, our junk will turn to gold — yet there are many for whom G-d decrees success *on condition* that they make a proper effort.

Thus even though Divine Providence directs all our steps in life, we have the privilege and the obligation to strive in natural ways to attain what we want.

Perhaps this is hinted in Hillel's words (*Avos* 1:14): "If I am not for myself, who will be for me? And if I am for myself, what am I?" If I don't take myself in hand and work at changing myself and improving my situation, who will do it for me? Who will remove the roadblocks that I set in my own way if I don't? On the other hand, if I think that I have achieved my successes through my own talents — what am I, anyway?

Let's accept blame for our failures and credit G-d with our successes.

Fail Well

More important than learning how to do well is learning how to fail well. Failures — lots of them — are inevitable. And paradoxically, the kernel of success is concealed within failure. The road to the summit is not at the top of the mountain; it is hidden down in the valley.

Yes, failure hurts. Maybe that is why many people equate failure with defeat. As soon as they stumble and fall, they give up.

This is a terrible mistake. Painful as it is, **failure is not defeat.** But whoever perceives it as such is defeated before he ever starts.

Look at Henry Ford. His Detroit Automobile Company, founded in 1899, closed a year later after building only twenty cars. Failure, yes; defeat, no. In 1901, he started the Henry Ford Company, which also failed. Do you think he was defeated? In 1903 he formed the Ford Motor Company, which made over 15 million Model T's by 1927.

It is virtually impossible to attain anything substantial without failing. Take the learning process of a small child. No person in the world is able to learn in a short time as much as an infant learns at the beginning of his life. He is born helpless; he doesn't understand the language his parents speak or the significance of the things he sees, and he cannot ask for what he wants. Within a very short time, he begins to pick up what is going on around him, understand his mother's language, recognize people close to him, identify objects, sit up, stand on his feet, and walk by himself. He practices and learns at an amazing pace.

Do you think it is easy to learn to sit on a chair without falling off? It takes the use of some three hundred different muscles! And what about learning to balance his body so as not to fall when he stands up, walks forward, or bends down to pick something up? Every movement requires an amazing combination of abilities!

Is there one thing that a child can learn without failing innumerable times? How often does he trip and fall, get up and try again until he learns to walk! How much practice goes into steering the spoon to his mouth without spilling most of its contents along the way! How much effort goes into getting a real word out of his mouth! Even if amused adults laugh at his failures, he will doggedly continue on. After hundreds of failures, he will bravely try again — with the same enthusiasm as the first time!

When we adults fail, we are embarrassed to try again. We quickly get frustrated, conclude that we lack the ability to succeed, and give up in despair.

Fortunately, little people don't yet have the "sense" to be embarrassed and to make such "logical" calculations. But woe is to us if our superior adult understanding undermines our chances to succeed!

The secret of success lies in the repeated efforts to over-come failures without despairing.

Winners don't know what defeat is. In every mistake they see a learning experience, in every failure a new opportunity, in every crisis a springboard. They know that the failure of some action doesn't make the person a failure.

Don't be afraid to fail! **Everyone has the right to try and also to fail.** The package deal of success includes many jarring failures. There is no opportunity without risk — "no risk, no gain" — and the greater the risk, the greater the opportunity for success. If you want to succeed, you need the courage to take risks and you must be prepared to fail.

Construction work is dirty. When a house is being built or renovated, even if it's a royal palace, the site looks as if it were hit by a tornado. It's full of dust, waste, and mud. When you go in, you get dirty, and your clothes are liable to get torn. It's upsetting, but there's no way to get the house you want without going through this difficult process.

At least when you build your house, you can hire workers and watch from a safe distance. But when you build your own self, you are the one who has to do the work. You can't build your self without "getting dirty," and you can't succeed without getting hurt occasionally.

Your Best Teacher

Failures are your best teachers. They are cues to make you aware of what you are doing wrong; analyze them calmly and carefully to see what things need improvement. Learn from your mistakes, keep moving toward your goal, and with G-d's help you will succeed in the end.

As a captain in the French and Indian War, George Washington made good use of his training in outdoor living. But he had no training in waging war or leading armies, and he made many mistakes. He built his fort on a small patch of open land surrounded by woods; the open land made the fort an easy target, while the woods shielded the enemy. Washington learned from his mistakes, made wiser choices in later battles, and went on to become a great general in the American Revolution.

So if you have failed, carefully analyze why you failed, what you did wrong. Fix it and try again. And again. *And again.* Don't give up. Only in this way can you succeed.

A friend tried to console Thomas Edison after his seven hundredth unsuccessful experiment with a storage battery. Edison replied, "Why, I have not failed. I've just found seven hundred ways that won't work."

That's a winner's approach. His actions may have failed — but *he* never did! Every failure advanced him toward his goal by teaching him what not to do.

Failure is an alarm that calls out, "There's something that you're doing wrong. Figure out what it is, change it, and get back on the road to success."

Cause and Effect

"Shallow people believe in luck and in circumstances," a great writer once said. "Strong people believe in cause and effect."

For every cause there is a result, and for every result there must be a cause. If there are raisins in the cake, someone must have put them there.

If no one put sugar into the coffee, the coffee will never be sweet — not even if you make the most aromatic coffee in the world, you pray, and you go to all the *gedolim* for blessings.

And if the milk is spoiled, then even if you try making coffee again and again, every cup will have the same problem.

Every result has a deed that preceded it, and every deed has a consequence. If I'm rude to my customers, people won't want to buy in my store. If people can't stand me, I must have done something that caused it. If I put on airs, I shouldn't be surprised that people don't take me seriously; if I want to impress others, that's exactly the impression I'll make. If I have a weak character and allow others to step on me, it's no wonder they do; it takes two to tango, and there are no exploiters without people who allow themselves to be exploited. If I'm afraid to say no to my children, it follows that my children will become more and more demanding.

If we continue to do tomorrow exactly what we did yesterday, the results will be the same. If we are not satisfied with what is happening in our lives, we need to check what we are doing to cause it. Nothing will change until we examine our deeds and change them.

Many people are afraid of change. They prefer their suffering, which is at least comfortably familiar. They may be frightened of the destruction of the old, something that may be necessary for rebuilding. Or they may lack the courage to admit to themselves that their behavior until now was wrong. No wonder people are reluctant to seek professional help.

If, for an individual, change may sometimes be a luxury that he is unwilling to pay for, in marriage it is a necessity. Some couples are worn out from years of conflict. Their home has turned into a Tower of Babel, where no one can communicate or agree about anything. But go to a marriage counselor? Heaven forbid! Do you think it's shame that holds them back? Unlikely, when all their neighbors, and sometimes also passersby, are aware of what's going on.

It was no secret that the Greens suffered greatly from marital conflict. Mr. Green asked me what to do about his son Motti, who had just been expelled from high school. I pointed out that for Motti's sake, he should see a marriage counselor.

"I know someone who went to a marriage counselor and it didn't help at all."

"Think for a minute," I said. "Someone who has a fatal disease will try anything to save himself. He won't give up because another fellow succumbed

despite treatment. Here the mental health of your whole family is at stake. Why are you looking for excuses to preserve the status quo?"

If you have failed until now to build a happy home or accomplish anything else, give up your comfortable old suffering! Muster the courage to get help if you need it (even this step may require counseling), make the necessary changes, and go forward to happiness and success.

Education

Today many youngsters are falling by the wayside because they aren't average. On one side are those who have difficulty keeping up and feel they aren't living up to society's expectations. On the other side are the superbright nonconformists who don't accept authority blindly. Both types, after repeated unsuccessful attempts to find their place, give up in despair. The results are liable to be tragic.

We can take measures to help prevent this. We must pay more attention to each child's individuality. We must teach our children and students how to live, how to cope with difficulties, and how to fail, pick themselves up, and keep going. And we must encourage them —

"Of course we encourage them!" many parents are probably saying right now. "When our children do what they're supposed to, boy, do we encourage them!"

Here's where the mistake lies. No one needs encouragement when things go right. One must encourage, support, and guide with understanding and empathy precisely when things go wrong. Ironically, just at that critical time, many parents send out negative messages. As a result, the child's self-confidence is eroded. He stops believing in himself and in his ability to ever succeed.

Never criticize or blame children when they don't succeed because of lack of know-how. Never make fun of children who fail in their efforts to do something. If you do, you will instill in them the belief that they must succeed on the first try. That is a terrible injustice; it is simply deception. Encourage them to fall and get up time after time without being embarrassed or dismayed.

Be supportive when your children fail. Encourage them when they're down, not just when they're up.

Don't teach your children and students only how to climb upward. Teach them how to stop and get down when necessary. Teach them how to fall without breaking their necks.

Teach them how to fail just as you teach them any other life skill. I hear youngsters who have hardly begun life saying, "What's the point in trying?" after they fail a few times. We must immunize children against the germs of bewilderment and despair to which they will be exposed after the fighting spirit of childhood dissipates.

Give your children the opportunity to make their own decisions, to make mistakes and learn from them.

Teach them that failure is only a cue to investigate what went wrong and whether a different approach is called for.

In this way, you prepare them for success in life.

A Hidden Blessing

Failure is a hidden blessing.

Failures are immunizations. They make us more mature, robust, and able to weather crises. G-d gives us setbacks so that we will grow through them.

People caught on a bridge that begins to collapse must muster all their strength and ingenuity to save themselves. Suddenly, they discover spiritual and physical resources they never knew they had.

Failure increases our chance to succeed by forcing us to choose new avenues.

A person who is doing all right becomes complacent. He is likely to stay in his position without advancing much. He is comfortable where he is, so why change and take risks? But if he falls, he will be forced to do something else in order to survive. He will have no choice but to change directions, take risks, and enter new fields.

Failure can indeed be frightening, and it may even threaten your whole way of life — but precisely then your ingenuity and life wisdom will find expression, and you may get much further than you ever dreamed possible.

Many who failed thought that the world had come to an end, but after adjusting to their new situation, they saw that Divine Providence had opened wonderful new vistas before them. If we look back at the failures we have suffered, we will often discover that they ultimately led to positive outcomes.

A simple Polish Jew named Yankel came to America and went out to look for work. Since he had no marketable skills, he applied for the position of shamash in a small local synagogue.

After a few days of trial, the gabbai of the synagogue decided to accept him for the position, to Yankel's great joy. A lengthy contract was prepared and he was asked to sign — but Yankel could not sign his name in English. They told him regretfully that they could not accept an illiterate for the job.

Yankel was very sad, but he did not despair. For lack of choice, he started selling rags from a pushcart. Success shone on him, and in a short time he had accumulated enough money to buy a second pushcart; then he opened a stand, and afterward a store. Before many years had passed, he became the wealthy owner of a chain of stores.

One day Yankel, accompanied by his lawyer, was about to complete a deal with an important compa-

ny. They were surprised to see him sign his name with an X. "It's amazing that a person who can't sign his name succeeded so phenomenally in business," they said. "Imagine what you would be if you could sign your name!"

Yankel smiled broadly. "If I could sign my name, today I would be a shamash in a small synagogue!"

Believe in Yourself

We have seen that in order for any deed to get done, it is necessary to have the will to do it. A child begins to speak because he wants to make his words heard, and takes his first steps because he wants to get places. We *do* because we *want* to do.

But will alone is not enough. In order for our will to move us to action, we need trust and belief in ourselves. We must trust ourselves to make the right decision and to move in the right direction; otherwise, we will flounder. Trust and belief go together; we can't trust a guard to protect us unless we believe that he has the power and the weapons to do so. And we can't trust ourselves unless we believe that we have the ability and the moral right to take action.

This is known as "self-confidence." It is what distinguishes between those who succeed and those who don't.

Self-confidence is the foundation of mental health.

A building can be renovated provided that its foundation is strong. You can even knock down an old structure and build a new one on top of the foundation as long as it is sound. But if the foundation is shaky, renovating the building is liable to destroy it. Before you attempt any renovations, you must first invest heavily in shoring up the foundation.

On a foundation of self-confidence you can build a healthy, mature, stable personality that can withstand strong winds. If you possess self-confidence, you will be able to work on self-improvement. You will be ready to go out and achieve any objective. You will approach each struggle in life with head held high. Even when the going gets rough, you won't entertain thoughts of giving up; you will pull yourself together and march briskly forward on the road to success.

A person who lacks self-confidence is like a container that is missing a bottom; it is pointless to put anything into it. All his efforts to succeed in life are liable to go to waste because he will crumble in the first storm.

Lack of self-confidence is one of the factors that prevent self-actualization. It can develop from many causes, but the result is fear of expressing your own feelings or opinions — lest they be wrong — and fear of doing what you want to do — lest there be a better way. It is paralyzing and destructive.

Make no mistake. Self-confidence does not mean that you think you know everything and can do anything. It means you are sure of your *right* to be yourself. It does not mean that you won't fail. It means you are not afraid that you might fail.

Like anything else, self-confidence is a relative term. Each of us has enough self-confidence to carry out certain actions, and not enough to do others. Regardless of where along the continuum we stand, there is always room for improving our self-confidence and mustering the courage to do something we hesitated to do in the past. And the more we develop our self-confidence, the more we will succeed in attaining our goals.

Moreover, a hefty dose of self-confidence is essential for navigating our way safely through life's various stages.

The Stages of Life

Just as we are pushed into the world, like it or not, so we are pushed forward in the tunnel of life, like it or not. This tunnel is divided into stages. At each stage we face new challenges that require new methods of coping. We must establish ourselves anew in our new setting and consolidate our inner forces in preparation for the next stage, where the process begins all over again.

Let's briefly scan some of the basic changes that most normal people go through.

Baby Yonah learns his place at home and somehow manages with his brothers and sisters — only to have his bliss disrupted by the birth of a newcomer. Yonah suddenly loses a portion of his parents' attention and is forced to adapt to a new place in the family hierarchy. When he finally adjusts at home, he is evicted for part of the day to a nursery school, where he must contend with dozens of children all vying for the same toys. No sooner does he learns to manage than he is thrown into first grade, where he must adapt to new friends and new rules. He is no longer allowed to play for long hours at a time. With every grade he goes up, the burden of study increases.

At last, eighth grade. Now Yonah is among the older boys, who feel they have made it to the top. But after passing through elementary school safely, can he rest on his laurels? No. Once again he is transferred to a strange, unfamiliar place: In high school, he has to start all over again from the bottom. And by the time he gets to the top in high school, he starts from the beginning at the next step in his education, or starts working, most likely at a low level as well.

Mazal tov! Yonah is engaged to be married! At last he will have a home of his own. Independence. No parents or teachers telling him what to do. No rules, no adapting. Freedom!

That's what *he* thinks. Reality soon sets in. With marriage, the *real* struggle for survival begins — and Yonah has no previous experience on which to draw.

First of all, he must learn to get along with his spouse. Yonah had thought he was marrying an angel, and one who would always agree with him. Now it turns out that Mrs. Yonah is a human being, and one with a will of her own to boot.

Add to this a mother-in-law. Plus a father-in-law. (Don't groan, Yonah. You'll be one, too, some day.) Not to mention the rest of Mrs. Yonah's family. They tell him gently, "When you were single, you were a free man. That's all over now!"

Here come the real decisions. Yonah must decide what he wants to work at and what he wants to achieve. He grapples with strong conflicts between the real and the ideal. It was easy to write checks on the bank account of dreams; now he must cover them. Zero hour has arrived: He must either fulfill his dreams or let go of them. The disappointments are many and unpleasant.

Children begin to arrive, and the pressure increases. Yonah has to work hard to support his family. With no previous experience, he (with Mrs. Yonah) must nevertheless become an expert in education; his children's lives are at stake! Each age brings new challenges: "little children, little problems; big children, big problems." How do you handle teenagers? Yonah has forgotten what it was like to be one himself.

With his children in *shidduchim*, Yonah (with his wife) must become an authority on how to find a spouse. He must negotiate with *mechutanim* and pay his share.

Mazal tov, Yonah. It was a beautiful wedding. How does it feel to be a father-in-law?

Now he must learn how to deal with married children and their spouses.

Ah, what a wonderful life! Zeidy Yonah heads a flourishing family and a thriving business. But what is this he sees in the mirror? A few hairs have turned white! Yonah is reminded that a certain time is approaching — a time when he will have to leave everything behind and account to his Maker for what he has done in life.

Yonah's hair is all white now, and he walks with a cane. If he lacks physical strength, at least he has the wisdom that comes with age and experience — but his children no longer consult him. Yonah feels like a burden to them. They're busy with their own lives, and do him a favor by visiting occasionally.

Sometimes we would rather return to the previous stage, which is familiar and comfortable. The little girl pleads with Mother to let her stay home instead of starting first grade. But any effort in this direction is simply a waste of energy. **There is no turning back!** Like it or not, we must keep moving ahead. You can't hold back time or return to yesterday any more than you can return an arrow to the quiver after it has been shot.

Someone who is not prepared to accept the changed personal reality is like a teenager who insists on wearing the same clothes he wore as a small child or like an old man who crosses a busy highway with horse and buggy because that's what he's used to. If one refuses to recognize change, it's no wonder he's beaten and hurt by it. Trying to live in a fantasy world can take a very high toll.

If we are pushed forward for better or for worse, we must accept the fact that there's no turning back. **Whenever life moves us to a new stage, we must bid farewell to the previous stage,** which was but is no longer. Painful though it may be, a woman of 50 must bid farewell to her childbearing years, and a man of 70 to his work years. The ability to close one chapter and open the next is absolutely vital.

There is no escaping reality; we have to face it squarely and deal with the new challenges it presents. Even death is less frightening when we accept its inevitability; I've used this principle in therapy and seen it bring relief. What determines whether we will be able to adjust to each new stage of life? Strength of character and faith in our ability to fight and to win — that is, self-confidence. This is so important that even people who feel confident and secure must constantly shore up and reinforce their self-confidence.

When the Going Gets Rough

If we need self-confidence when the tunnel of life is smooth, all the more so when the going gets rough.

For instance, if an unhealthy child is born, family life and the daily routine change. Everything begins to revolve around this child and his special needs. This is taxing enough if both parents see eye to eye on how to cope. But what happens when each wants to deal with the situation differently?

Even someone fortunate enough to have a positive self-image has no guarantee that he will continue to feel self-confident all his life. Even the strongest among us are liable to find themselves laid flat by a drastic, unexpected event.

Mr. Katz was a wealthy philanthropist, highly respected in his community. When the bottom fell out of the stock market, he suddenly lost his wealth. The new reality forced him to be frugal with expenditures and even take loans. His prestige in society plummeted. He became frustrated and nervous — which affected domestic harmony and even had a negative effect on his children.

Life is incredibly complex. No one knows what lurks at the next turn. From the cradle to the grave, we have no rest and no possibility of evading life's hardships. "Man was born to toil" (*Iyov* 5:7).

To win a war, you prepare ahead of time. You assess the situation and, carefully weighing each step, plan your strategy and try to outguess the enemy. You stockpile weapons, build an army, and train your troops. Then, on the battlefield, you strive to implement your plans and deploy your men and weapons cleverly.

But in life, we frequently have to plan strategies while the battle is raging and build an arsenal of spiritual strength under fire. Sometimes we need to rebuild our fortress while bombs are falling on our heads and the earth is shaking beneath our feet.

No one is born with everything he needs to cope with life's difficulties. We all come into an existing world, like aliens coming to live in a strange city. Some are born into comfortable, supportive surroundings; others are thrown into a cold, hostile environment. Some arrive well equipped, whole in body and mind; others are handicapped. Regardless of how we start out, we must learn to manage on our own and to keep our heads above water in every situation.

Unlike in war, there is no possibility of ending the battles with one decisive victory and then enjoying peace. In real life, there is no rest and there is no possibility of having everything go our way. Divine Providence pitches people into situations that shake them up physically, spiritually, or ideologically. Although we have the power to do and change much in all areas of life, "many designs are in a man's heart; but only Hashem's counsel will prevail" (*Mishlei* 19:21).

No one is the master of his own physical health or that of his family. We cannot control other people. We cannot even be sure that we will always have bread. On the spiritual front, our worst enemy of all — the indefatigable evil inclination — continually changes disguises and tactics in his relentless war against us. Reality can be stranger than fiction, and we don't know what the future holds.

We must be ready to cope courageously with life's vicissitudes and adapt to every new situation. Only if we fortify ourselves appropriately with self-confidence, and feel certain of our ability to cope, will we be able, with G-d's help, to weather crises and remain strong and stable.

Since self-confidence is so pivotal to success in life, let's take a deeper look at what makes it or breaks it and what one can do to improve it.

Where Did Our Self-Confidence Go?

Reuven is strong and self-confident; you might even call him shock-resistant. He knows how to deal with difficulties and emerge from crises as a winner. Shimon is weak and timid; whenever he encounters a problem, he becomes frightened and loses control.

Reuvens and Shimons are everywhere; we all know many of each. The tremendous difference between the two types is astounding — especially when we find both personalities in ourselves! In certain circumstances we are Reuvens, in others, Shimons.

Both Reuven and Shimon were born chock full of self-confidence. How do I know? Just look at how much courage, daring, and strength of character babies have! Despite their weakness and limitations, they seem to be totally confident that they can do above and beyond what we adults think. Watch a child as he takes his first step. He swaggers like a drunkard and falls again and again, but these failures don't deter him. With stubborn determination, he keeps on trying until he succeeds in mastering the skill of walking.

Learning to feed himself is another demanding feat. First he fights Mother for the spoon. Then he works hard to put the spoon into the bowl, and afterward to trap some food. Next comes the difficult journey through the air to the goal. Again and again he loses the precious contents along the way, but innumerable failures don't daunt him. Finally, the last stretch: getting spoon into mouth. Mother is exhausted; bystanders laugh; highchair, hair, and bib are soiled, and perhaps also the floor. But Baby has a triumphant grin on his dirty face.

What happened to the self-confidence we had in child-hood? How many of us are capable today of going back to something that we failed at dozens of times, and take another crack at it as enthusiastically as if it were our first try? Where has all our courage gone? How did our self-confidence become eroded?

And how did Shimon grow up to be so much more timid than Reuven?

The Memory Bank

All our experiences, from early childhood through old age, are permanently stored in our memory. Without our necessarily being aware of the process, whenever we face a new situation, our mind automatically scans the memory, calls up similar events from the past, and compares them with the new situation. If the old events left a good impression on us, we will expect to feel the same way in our new situation. But if the old events left us with a bad taste and hurt feelings, we will expect unpleasant feelings and we will be afraid. **These expectations to a large measure determine what will actually happen.**

If we were held up to public ridicule after we tried to stand up for our rights, we will not hurry to do it again. But if we stood up for our rights and won, we will take bold risks next time. We have learned that effort pays off. Our past success, stored in our memory, will promote more success. That is how **failure begets failure, and success begets success.**

Let's examine the deposits made in our memory bank as we were growing that affected the development of our self-confidence. We will look at adaptation, nurturing, and the struggle for independence.

Adaptation

We follow a toddler on his first day in nursery, as he encounters a strange new world with which he must learn to cope. For the first time, he comes up against fixed social rules. Instead of one or two siblings who pull away his toys, or one loving, compassionate mother with whom he has to negotiate over a cookie, he is now forced to deal with dozens of children, all vying for status and toys. Although the teacher tries hard to keep order and protect the weak, there is still some merciless use of elbows.

During the first few days, the children are frightened and confused. They don't know what to make of this new world into which they have been thrown. Some weep at first over the loss of the security of their warm, loving homes, but little by little become stronger and catch on to the rules of the game. Others feel lost and withdraw into their shells. Some wage a spirited fight over their turfs. Others try but fail, and end up surrendering to those who are stronger.

Moishie decided that he wanted the red crayon, which happened to be in Yitzie's hand. Yitzie tried with all his might to hold on to it, but Moishie overpowered him while the teacher wasn't looking. Yitzie was not the type to complain, and Moishie enjoyed his victory. Similar incidents followed in rapid succession, and Moishie quickly learned from experience that force works; he could succeed in getting his way by fighting for what he wanted. As for the defeated Yitzie, the next time he fought for his rights, his knees trembled. He knew from experience that he would fail — and he did, reinforcing his belief that he was a weakling. He turned passive, reacting only when there was no choice, and then only halfheartedly.

In this way, small deposits are made in our memory bank. As they accumulate, they become a determining factor in our lives.

Nurturing
Many of the deposits in our memory bank are made by our parents and teachers.

All future traits and skills exist in potential in a person from infancy. A baby's personality is like the ingredients in a mixing bowl. All breads and pastries are based on flour and liquid with some additions, but stone-ground whole-wheat flour and apple juice yield a different product than does white flour and water. By mixing, kneading, leaving to rise, and shaping, you can bake many different varieties of breads, cookies, cakes, and pies.

A baby has all the basic ingredients, but these have not yet been processed. During his first years, his parents begin to help him develop his talents, shape his outlook, balance his emotions, and control his drives. The result will be obtained only after the "baking," when he grows up and his personality is formed.

Actually, for a human being there is no moment of "baking." All of us continue to develop until our last day on earth. We will always encounter new situations, and we must constantly adapt ourselves anew. Moreover, although it becomes harder as we get older, we can always change. But the basis is formed in childhood.

For some children, childhood goes smoothly and quietly; all needs are filled adequately by encouraging, supportive parents and teachers. This provides a warm atmosphere in which their personality and emotions can develop properly. Quite different is the child who is raised and educated in a cold, tense environment, with parents who hit him more than necessary, and harsh teachers, or rough classmates. He is liable to resemble dough that wasn't kneaded properly and didn't have a chance to rise in warm air before being put into the oven.

The Struggle for Independence

A third type of deposit made in our memory bank is the result of the struggle for independence.

From the day a child first opens his eyes, he is at the bottom looking up. He lies in his crib helpless; others feed, clean, and change him. Later on, he crawls on the floor and looks up at others walking erect and with ease. At the table, he struggles with the spoon and watches others maneuvering knife and fork with aplomb. To him, the buttons on his shirt pose a major challenge, while he sees others getting dressed quickly and efficiently.

He spends almost all his waking hours every day learning and practicing skills in order to catch up with others and raise his status. Valiantly he works his way up in life, with a willpower seldom found among adults.

But at the same time, his parents are there to help; he can rely on them to devotedly fill his needs. This frees him from the burden of responsibility. If ever he feels incapable of carrying out a mission, whether self-imposed or assigned to him by others, Mother is sure to come to his rescue.

The child is buffeted between two opposing forces within him. On the one hand, his desire to be *big* drives him to perform new and difficult feats that test the limits of his abilities; on the other hand, he has a natural wish to sit back and enjoy having his work done by others because he is still small.

Which way will he go? Will he choose the hard way — mustering courage and striding confidently into the unknown? Or will he choose the easy, safe way out — giving up at the first sign of difficulty, and asking others to do the work for him?

Parents and teachers play a key role in the child's deciding between the two.

Some educators imbue the child with faith in his own ability. They consistently encourage him not to give up. When he fails, they urge him to try again and again until he succeeds; and when he does, they praise him lavishly. The child learns that effort pays; it brings success and praise. Every challenge that he overcomes reinforces this positive approach and increases his self-confidence. He will continue to grow and work hard to overcome difficulties. The statements he gets from his memory bank tell him, "You're a winner! You can do it!"

But in some families, when a child puts his right shoe on the left foot, parents pounce on him: "*Shlemiel!* You never do anything right!" Even worse, they may torment him by saying, "How come Avi can do it and you can't?" All this is recorded permanently in his memory. Such comments, if repeated consistently, deal deadly blows to his self-confidence. In the course of time the child will begin to believe that he is not only unsuccessful, but also inferior to normal children. He will go through life beaten and humiliated, always wondering where the next blow will come from. He "knows" from experience that all his attempts will inevitably end in failure and disappointment. The statements he gets from his memory bank say, "You're not as good as the others."

Nineteen-year-old Yaakov Rubin was convinced that his facial features were abnormal. Although he was a good student of fine character, he was sure that there was something wrong with him and that he didn't fit into society.

In our sessions, I learned that when Yaakov was little, he had been slower moving than his siblings. In order to liven him up, Mr. Rubin would mimic his son's slow motions. Once Mr. Rubin pointed to a retarded man and told Yaakov, "That's how you're going to look when you grow up if you don't change now." Instead of changing in the direction his father wanted, Yaakov became a loner, convinced that he was abnormal.

"If Dad, who is smart and successful, diagnosed this abnormality in me," Yaakov told me, "then he must be right and I certainly won't be able to change. Finished."

"Your father is wrong," I said. "You believed him because you lost your self-confidence, just as anyone who has been criticized systematically would."

At first, Mr. Rubin objected to my approach. He wanted me to explain to Yaakov that he was not behaving properly and that was why he reacted as he did. Fortunately, I managed to convince Mr. Rubin that to get results, I needed to help his son regain his lost self-confidence. It was important not to focus on who was guilty but on what needed to be done.

When Yaakov finally understood what had happened, I told him the time had come to test reality — and the only way was by going out among people and speaking with them. Although it would be hard at first, it would get easier with practice.

As usual, success brought success. Little by little, Yaakov overcame his problem.

Believe it or not, pampering and overprotecting convey to a child that he is incapable of doing anything properly, no less than putting him down would. Spoiling a child by giving him whatever his heart desires and trying to cushion him from the bumps on the road of childhood say, "You can't manage on your own." So does making all the child's decisions for him: determining what he should wear, which friends he should invite over, what games he should play. Pampering and dictating destroy the child's mental independence and prevent him from learning to make his own decisions. As a result, he will lack the boldness to cope independently with life's challenges and will always need the guidance and approval of others.

The nearest yeshivah high school was so far from home that Yehoshua had no choice but to dorm. From the beginning, he complained that he was homesick and simply couldn't sleep in the dormitory. He tried to manage, but sometimes had panic attacks in the middle of the night. His parents turned to me for help.

It turned out that Yehoshua had been pampered and overprotected to such an extent that he had never even gone into a shoe store; his father would bring new shoes home for him. I explained to the parents that Yehoshua needed to be weaned of his dependence on them and learn to deal with the world.

Yehoshua's parents learned how to set firm limits. They informed him that they would speak to him no more than once a day, and that he could not go home whenever he wanted. I warned them that Yehoshua would test the limits, and he did. It wasn't easy, but they were ready and knew how to cope.

Before long, they told me they were delighted by the changes in Yehoshua. He had become more self-confident and had begun to cope well with his own difficulties.

Don't Blame Others

"Aha!" you say. "Now I know why I lack self-confidence! It's all my parents' fault!"

Never blame your parents or teachers, if only because it's a waste of time; you won't gain anything from it.

Why, then, should I inform you about improper child rearing methods? So that you will know that your lack of self-confidence is not an unchangeable, inborn trait. It's merely a mistake in your upbringing, which can be corrected!

We alone are responsible for our lives. It's up to us to overcome our weaknesses. And that is easier to do when we know we weren't born that way.

Our self-confidence and courage were dealt many blows until they became damaged, and now we must learn how to heal them.

Let go of the past. It doesn't matter what happene
up until today. Resolve that from this moment on,
invest whatever it takes to build a positive self-imɛ
acquire a positive, confident approach to life, which v
you to success.

Ask yourself:

- How did my self-confidence disappear?
- What failures and pressures led me to retreat?
- Did I choose to evade and escape instead of coping
  and fighting?

If you succeed in reconstructing what happened, you will
see that every failure left you more unsure of yourself and
more hesitant to take risks, which led to even greater failure,
in a vicious cycle.

To break the negative cycle is hard. But there's an easier
way to undo the damage.

Develop a positive cycle!

How?

Focus on your successes, and only on your successes. Pat
yourself on the back any time you have even the smallest
success. In this way, you will gradually bolster your faith in
yourself and in your ability to succeed, and simultaneously
diminish your self-doubt. Your increased self-confidence will
improve your chances of success, and every success will feed
your self-confidence, in an upward spiral.

Another approach is to view timidity as a bad habit, and
habits can be broken. In the coming chapter, we will take a
deeper look at habits and how to break them.

Break
Your Bad Habits

How do we acquire habits?

Presumedly, we don't do things unless we have a reason to. Behind every habit is an urge that caused us to acquire and strengthen the habit. It's only logical — straightforward cause and effect. Right?

Wrong.

Cause and effect, yes; straightforward, no. Because the moment we do something in response to any urge, cause and effect switch roles! The action itself turns into the dominant cause, and the urge becomes the natural result. Each action strengthens and intensifies the urge that led to it.

Sheila couldn't resist the urge to clean. For many hours each day, she walked around the house with a dust cloth, removing mostly imaginary dust from her *furniture like a windshield wiper that can't be turned off. She was exhausted from the effort, and didn't know what to do about it.*

The more Sheila gave in to her drive, the stronger it became, and the weaker her ability to resist it. So the more Sheila dusted, the more she needed to dust. True, this is an example of obsessive-compulsive disorder (see Chapter 24), but the same applies to any habit.

The principle is: *Acharei hamaasim nimshachim halevavos,* **Our hearts are drawn after our actions** (*Sefer HaChinuch,* mitzvah 16).

One of the habits that work this way is fear.

All fears and phobias, from being embarrassed to enter a synagogue late to being afraid to go into an elevator, begin to develop after a person retreats in an attempt to evade unpleasantness. The trouble is that instead of bringing about the hoped-for relief, the retreat intensifies his fears and worries, and with it his suffering.

A ri was afraid of dogs. One morning as Ari was walking to school, a dog without a leash came toward him. Ari ran into the gutter to escape.

The act of fleeing reinforced Ari's fear. The next time he encountered a dog, he felt an even stronger urge to flee.

Any action taken in response to fear intensifies the fear, which influences future actions, which intensify the fear. In other words, by acting out of fear, you increase your fear.

Break the Cycle

How can we break this vicious cycle?

By using the same principle: Our hearts are drawn after our actions. Any time we don't give in to a certain urge, we weaken it.

Sheila resolved to control herself and let the dust settle for a while. At first it was difficult. But eventually the urge to clean weakened, and she found it easier to control the urge than to do all that dusting.

❖   ❖   ❖

Avi decided he was going to be brave. The next time he encountered a dog, he continued walking, though his heart pounded with fear. After that, it became easier to stand his ground.

This principle can help us greatly to improve a character trait or change a habit, such as reacting impulsively or speaking *lashon hara*. It is certainly the most effective and perhaps the only way to overcome fear.

Fear is what lies behind all lack of self-confidence: fear of rejection, fear of being laughed at, or fear of failing. A person who lacks self-confidence behaves in a certain way because he fears what might happen if he behaves the other way. Thus he acquires the habit of sitting back and doing nothing. He chooses silence when he should speak, inaction when deeds are called for, and surrender to exploitation when he should assert his rights. He doesn't notice that refraining from risks only intensifies his fear and weakens him even more.

As a first step toward bolstering your self-confidence, resolve firmly that you will not give in to fears and worries. **Do what you fear to do.** Instead of waiting until you feel more confident, take bold action now.

Don't get me wrong. I don't expect you to become a hero overnight. One of the secrets of success is to proceed gradually.

The Method

Here's a method I've used to help many people overcome various fears and phobias:

- Write down a precise goal that you want to achieve.
- List clearly defined actions you will take to achieve it.
- Break them down into small, clearly defined sub-actions.
- Number all the sub-actions in order of increasing difficulty. Number 1 on your list should be a small step that you feel ready for. Number 2 should be only slightly more difficult.
- Now start working. Practice number 1 for a while until you become used to it and find it easy. Then put a check next to number 1 and go on to number 2.

Of course, even number 1 demands some courage, but there is no alternative. G-d "gives wisdom to the wise" (*Daniel* 2:21). You must somehow muster a little courage to begin the process, and then G-d will help you move forward. "Open for Me an opening like the eye of a needle, and I will make an opening for you as wide as a hall" (see *Shir HaShirim Rabbah* 5:3).

When Mendel needed to talk to strangers, he would become so nervous and frightened that he couldn't ask a simple question.

"What do you think will happen if you ask a stranger for the time?" I asked him.

"I'll sound silly. People will laugh at me."

"How would you react if someone were to ask you for the time?" I continued. "Would you think he was silly? Would you laugh at him?"

"Of course not."

"So on what basis did you conclude that people would see you as silly?"

Mendel began to see that his feelings were not facts; his feeling silly didn't prove that others would think he was. He came to realize that the only way to find out how people would react was by trying it.

I explained the principle that "our hearts are drawn after our actions" and handed him a notebook and pen. Together we drew up a plan of action. Mendel wrote:

Goal: To feel comfortable talking to strangers.

Actions: Go over to strangers and start talking to them.

Sub-actions:

1. Go up to a stranger in the street and ask, "What time is it?"
2. Go up to a stranger and ask, "Where is Main Street?"
3. Go into a store that sells something I want to buy and ask the salesman about prices.

It took several sessions before Mendel mustered the courage to perform step 1. He practiced for a while until it became easy for him. Then he graduated to step 2. He continued until he felt comfortable talking to strangers.

The process can be very hard, and sometimes you will have to enter into situations that you find scary. But ultimately you will get used to the new situation. Just remember to start with small steps, and increase the difficulty only when you are ready.

If you persist in your efforts and gradually increase the risks you are willing to take, in the course of time you will see yourself doing things that brave, self-confident people do. You, too, will be one of them. If you actually do what you fear, you will overcome that fear.

Act confident, and you will become confident.

Small Changes, Big Revolutions

hy do people find it so hard to change? Let's listen to what they say.

"I tried to change. I decided to become a different person, but it didn't last."

People think that changing means turning into somebody else. An angry person wants to turn into a calm one, an impulsive person into a deliberate one, a spiteful person into a loving one. Such goals, admirable as they appear to be, are usually doomed to failure from the outset. They are too difficult, if not impossible to achieve. The approach is simply wrong.

"Of course it didn't last," I tell them. "The reason is simple. You can't suddenly become a different person. All you can do is make a small change — and *that* will turn you into a different person."

The principle is that **big revolutions come from small changes**.

In mathematics and exact science, everything is counted, calculated, weighed, and measured. The results are independent of an individual's world outlook or his mood. One and one is two, ten minus one is nine. Only the quantity matters; quality is irrelevant. If I'm counting eggs, the eggs themselves stay the same as they were — large or small, fresh or stale, raw or cooked. Only the quantity changes. And quantity is exact, absolute.

But when it comes to the emotional and spiritual parts of our lives, or to our effectiveness, what matters is quality. Here mathematics breaks down. The whole becomes greater than the sum of its parts; one plus one is much greater than two.

The power of the prayers or mitzvos of a group of twenty, for instance, is much greater than that of twenty individuals. "The three-ply cord is not quickly severed" (*Koheles* 4:12) — the strength of a three-ply cord is much greater than the total strength of three individual cords.

"If you will follow My decrees ... five of you will pursue 100, and 100 of you will pursue 10,000, and your enemies will fall before you by the sword" (*Vayikra* 26:3-8). "What happened to the calculations?" asks *Rashi*. If five righteous Jews rout 100 enemies, then 100 should rout only 2,000. Instead, the Torah suddenly boosts the ratio from 1:20 to 1:100!

"There is no comparison," replies *Rashi*, "between a few who obey the Torah, and many who obey the Torah."

On the mundane level, the difference between one-half cup of water and a whole cup is quantitative. But when Mrs. Miller put an extra tablespoon of salt into the pot, the quality of the whole soup changed; the whole thing became too salty.

A messy kitchen is not measured by the number of items that are out of place. A pile of dirty dishes may contribute more to the appearance of mess than is warranted by the number of dishes in the pile.

If a doctor makes a mistake — well, it happens. But if he makes a mistake again the next day, doubt is cast on his professional capability. Here one plus one adds up to much more than two.

Why did the proverbial straw break the camel's back? Surely not because of the weight of one more piece of straw! That unlucky straw combined qualitatively with the entire load that was already on the camel's back. That's how pressure works. Looking at it from the positive side: If you have ten problems that worry you, and you solve one, the relief you gain is much greater than 10 percent. The nine that remain become a much lighter load.

Our personality is made up of a composite of characteristics and tendencies. Any change, small as it may be, affects the whole composite. The slightest change in our way of life or behavior shakes up our whole personality. It's like mixing a few drops of white into black paint. Instead of black, you have a new color — gray.

Using the Principle

How can we make the principle of small changes work for us?

Suppose your 13-year-old daughter refuses to help with the housework. If you get her to agree to merely straighten up her own bedroom, at least she will no longer be someone who "doesn't do a thing at home." Before long, she will help in other ways as well.

A wife complains that her husband ignores her. Demands to change completely will evoke total opposition. But the couple might work out an agreement to spend half an hour together in the evening without answering phones or reading newspapers, or to go out for an hour or two every other week. This little change can transform their marriage, for once any change is made in their lives, they are no longer in the same place they were before. Their feelings will change, making it easier for them to continue improving their relationship.

This is tested and proven.

If a meal is placed before a very hungry person, can he eat all of it at one shot? Of course not. The biggest feast can only be eaten one bite at a time. Spoonful after spoonful, forkful after forkful, and eventually the stomach is full.

Just as prisoners have dug tunnels to freedom by scooping out dirt bit by bit, so, too, can we uproot our bad habits by working on them bit by bit.

If a yeshivah student has no desire to learn, what will happen if his *mashgiach* demands that he take himself in hand and turn into a *masmid*? Except in a rare case, the boy simply won't be able to do it. I would urge him to make one small change of his choice, such as studying a mere 10 minutes at the beginning of every *seder*. The point is to get him working on self-improvement. The first small change will affect his whole self-image and propel him forward. Experiencing even a little success catalyzes further change and more success.

If someone lacks self-confidence, I might ask him to refuse one exploitive request or to make one comment when he is with friends. If he keeps this up every day for a week, in a short time he will undergo a mighty transformation.

Imagine that you are standing midway up a hill and looking at beautiful scenery. For every few inches higher that you go, the whole view changes — because the scenery is more than another square yard of land or two more trees.

Shimi was the terror of the dormitory. He hit the other boys; in the lunchroom, he threw spoons and food.

"I've tried to stop," Shimi told me. "But I've always failed. My good resolutions don't hold up long."

"Here's what I want you to do," I told him. "Pick any meal you want. At that meal, for 15 minutes, you *will restrain yourself. No matter what happens, you won't react, you won't throw anything. Which meal do you choose?"*

"I'll take lunch. But 15 minutes is a joke. If I can start throwing things after 15 minutes, what's it worth?"

"It's true that 15 minutes isn't a lot," I said. "But for my part, after you've restrained yourself for 15 minutes you can do whatever you want. All I need is for you to fill out a chart that I'll give you about how you exercised self-control for 15 minutes every day when you went to lunch, for one week. That's all."

"Okay," said Shimi. "That's easy enough."

A week later he reported that he had continued to restrain himself beyond the agreed-upon 15 minutes. By the time two months had passed, Shimi had stopped throwing things altogether.

"The journey of a thousand miles begins with a single step," says an ancient Chinese proverb. Take the first step to change right now. That first step will impact your whole quality of life. And the next step will be easier.

Watch Your Diction

"**I** can't control the urge to smoke," a chain smoker told me.

"If you were given $20 a day to go through the day without smoking, would you stop?" I asked.

"No," he said. "I told you I can't stop."

"And if you got $200?"

"Oh." He hesitated, and a smile spread over his face. "That's another story.

So why do you say 'I can't'?" I told him. "You yourself admit that you can; you just don't have a strong enough reason for doing it. From now on, say, 'I don't have enough of a reason to stop smoking.' "

There are many ways to work on evaluating your ability correctly. The simplest is to use words accurately.

Often we say "We can't" when we mean "It's hard for me to." You *can't* hold your breath for an hour or jump up five stories even if someone paid you a million dollars to do it or threatened to kill you if you didn't. On the other hand, it may be *hard* to stop being lazy or to control your temper, but it is not impossible. When you feel that you absolutely must, you will surprise yourself by doing things you thought you couldn't.

"When I get upset," said Nat, "I can't control myself. So I use my hands."

"What do you mean by 'I can't control myself'?" I asked.

"I mean that I don't know what I'm doing."

"Has it ever happened that when you got angry, you stabbed someone with a knife?"

"Heaven forbid." Nat was aghast at the thought. "Do I look to you like a murderer?"

"Did you ever break someone's eyeglasses in your anger?"

"No!"

"Did you ever put yourself in danger by beating up a fellow who was much bigger and stronger than you?"

"Do you think I'm stupid? Hey, what are you getting at with all these questions?"

"How can it be that when you 'can't control' yourself, you still know exactly what not to do?"

If ever you find yourself about to do something you shouldn't do, and you feel you can't control yourself, ask yourself, "Would I do this if people were watching? Would I do it in front of a camera?" If the answer is no, you *can* control yourself. And it's not the people or the camera that overcome your drive; they only help you decide to restrain yourself. (You obviously cannot stop yourself from falling if you slip on ice just because it is embarrassing.) Ultimately, regardless of your reason, what stops you is your own decision.

I have worked with many youngsters whose main problem was that they were convinced they couldn't do anything about their problems. A taped message in their heads told them "You can't." Whether this message was recorded by them or by the adults around them, it took a lot of work to convince them to even try.

Motti, who had serious discipline problems, claimed he couldn't take responsibility for his actions. In our sessions he kept saying, "I can't control myself," "I can't improve," and "I'll never amount to anything."

I knew that this was not so, but couldn't find out where he got this idea — until one day he mentioned that his teacher had gotten very angry and called him "a lost cause."

"How does this teacher try to encourage you to study?" I asked.

Motti replied, "He tells me all the time that I'm not normal and I'm not responsible for my actions, and if I don't do something to stop my wild behavior, I'm going to end up in a mental asylum."

At last we had gotten to the bottom of the problem! The rest was relatively simple. I explained to the teacher that Motti had internalized destructive messages until he believed that he was no good. In order to help him, we would have to record an opposite message by expressing more faith in Motti than Motti had in himself.

The new approach paid off. The boy who ha
nalized the message "I can't improve" began to
and eventually prove, that he could.

Someone who constantly proclaims "I can't" is actively brainwashing himself that it is beyond his ability. He himself is sabotaging his chances of becoming what he wants to be, because if he "can't" he won't even try; and if he won't try it, he has no chance of succeeding. He slams the door to success in his own face.

So choose your words carefully. Don't say "I can't" when you mean something different. Get into the habit of saying, "I don't have sufficient reason to," "It's hard for me," "I'm afraid that," "I'm worried about." Speaking this way supports the feeling that you can change if you want to. It opens the door to overcoming the difficulty, fear, and worries.

When you believe that you can do something, you will make the required efforts, and you will undoubtedly succeed. This success will in turn reinforce your conviction that indeed you can succeed.

Tell yourself again and again: **Many things that seem to be beyond my ability are really not.** G-d has given us amazing capabilities, and we are able to do much more than we think.

Be Humble,
not "Humble"

"I'm afraid you're trying to make me arrogant."
Here I was trying to help Michael build up his self-confidence, and that was his reaction. I realized that in order to feel comfortable with his feeling of inferiority, he had begun to see it as "humility." In his own eyes, he had become a tzaddik; his weakness would get him a front seat in the World to Come. With this he consoled himself — and avoided the work of improving!

I asked Michael to help me make a list of characteristics found in an arrogant person, and those found in a humble one. The list looked like this:

ARROGANT	HUMBLE
Must show that he's perfect	Isn't afraid someone will discover that he's imperfect
Doesn't tolerate criticism	Is happy to receive criticism
Won't admit personal weakness	Isn't ashamed of his personal weakness
Preoccupied with thoughts of how to impress others and hide his own faults	Is barely concerned about what others think of him; doesn't think about whether he is appreciated enough
Sees anyone who is more successful than he as a threat	Is not concerned if others are more successful
Tries to show everyone that he is better than they are	Doesn't feel a need to prove his superiority

"Now, Michael, let's check where a person who feels inferior and lacks self-confidence fits into this picture."

The key difference between an arrogant person and a humble one is what's on his mind. I once heard a good definition: Humility is not that you think less of yourself; it's that you think of yourself less.

This aptly describes the person with healthy self-confidence. He is not preoccupied with his self-image and what others think of him. You can find in him all the characteristics of the humble.

In contrast, someone who lacks self-confidence is always thinking about what others think of him. His characteristics match those of the arrogant.

To take it a step further: A humble person has healthy self-confidence, whereas an arrogant one has feelings of inferiority.

A person with feelings of inferiority is frustrated by his weakness. A humble person lives a calmer life. He is happy with himself; he doesn't waste time wondering how others see him. He does what he must without the endless deliberations of people who suffer from feelings of inferiority.

Go over the two lists and ask yourself: Am I humble or am I "humble"?

Misconceptions

Yeshayah studied Talmud with great diligence and deep understanding, and he had wonderful character traits. But he got upset if people said so — for fear of arrogance — and tried to convince himself that they were mistaken.

"I don't learn well at all," he told me. As for character, "Well, that's because I'm quiet by nature." When I tried to point out something special that he did, he said quickly, "Everyone would have done the same."

Had Yeshayah reacted the same way to his shortcomings, fine. But he blew those up way out of proportion, and knocked down only his virtues. Instead of following our Sages' recommendation, "Judge the whole person favorably" (Avos 1:6), he judged his whole self unfavorably.

Since Yeshayah really was a diligent youth of strong character, his repeated efforts to be "humble" succeeded — he became nervous, tense, and confused. He didn't know where the truth began and the lie ended.

"Is it possible that our holy Torah, which praises the humble, commands a person to live a lie?" I asked Yeshayah. "If someone has wisdom or talent, he's lying if he claims it isn't true. It's forbidden to disrespect himself or to lie. Instead, he should praise Hashem for granting him these blessings."

If humility required us to think we're worthless fools, how could the great, humble Sages of Israel have ever accepted the responsibility of deciding fateful questions? When people came to consult them, why didn't they respond in surprise, "Why are you coming to ask me? I'm ignorant. Go find someone else!"

Our Sages knew the truth and did not deny it. They used their wisdom to guide those who sought their help. Their humility was expressed in not looking down on others and in ascribing their greatness to G-d's kindness.

The Gemara relates (*Pesachim* 106a) that when R' Ashi came to Mechoza, he was honored with reciting *Kiddush* for the congregation on Shabbos morning. R' Ashi did not know whether the local custom was to recite only the blessing over wine, or also the blessing of sanctification (*mekadesh haShabbos*), as at night. So he recited the blessing over wine, drawing out the last word to see what would happen. When he saw one of the listeners begin to drink from his cup, R' Ashi knew that one blessing sufficed. Seeing that his tactic had succeeded, R' Ashi said of himself, "The wise man has his eyes in his head" (*Koheles* 2:14).

It is said that when the Chasam Sofer received a letter that saluted him as "Rabbi of the whole Diaspora," he wept and said, "It's true, but woe to the generation that has someone like me at its helm!"

Those who get tangled up while working on their humility must look for the way out, in the direction of arrogance. If they had no arrogance in them, they wouldn't be perturbed by thoughts of humility. They simply wouldn't measure themselves against others at all.

A humble person does not feel the need to deny sincere compliments. He accepts himself, tries to improve whatever needs improvement, and recognizes his good points without taking credit for himself or looking down at others.

"It's Nothing"

A foolish but widespread mistake is that when someone is given a compliment, he thinks he has to put himself down. He hastily says, "Oh, it's nothing," as if he were obligated to apologize for anything good that he has done.

"You're welcome" would satisfy the rules of etiquette. "It's nothing" is usually an out-and-out lie, and both sides know it. And how does it make the thanker feel? You wanted your friend to accept your heartfelt gratitude, and he responds with phony etiquette! If it's a truly good friend, try reacting to "It's nothing" with "You're right, you don't have thanks coming to you for this" — and just watch how insulted he gets!

> *After hearing a chazzan pray beautifully, I went over and told him how much I had enjoyed his praying.*
>
> *"Oh," he replied, "it wasn't all that good."*
>
> *I sniffed the lie in his words, so I said, "Maybe you're right. I'm not such a connoisseur of chazanus."*
>
> *His initial reaction was to take offense. But after he recovered from the shock, the chazzan thanked me and said, "You've just taught me how to accept a compliment."*

A person who rebuffs compliments and puts down his every virtue is not working on character improvement and is not humble. He is simply in error, and he is hurting rather than helping himself, even when he speaks this way for the sake of etiquette.

Before praying, Rebbe Elimelech of Lyzhensk would ask G-d to let "each of us see our friend's virtues and not his flaws," but there is no supplication for seeing only our own flaws and not our virtues. R' Yisrael Salanter said, "A person who does not know what his own flaws are does not know what he must fix. But if he does not know his strong points, he does not know what tools he has for fixing.

Education

"My teenage son Yoel is no longer interested in studying," Mr. Weber said. "To make it worse, he's gotten in with a crowd of bad friends."

I asked about his child-raising methods. "I made sure he didn't develop arrogance," Mr. Weber told me proudly. "I systematically burst the bubbles of every good thing he did."

"Can you give me a specific example?" I asked.

He thought a minute. "When Yoel was 10 he once came home from school very excited. He had gotten a 95 on a test. 'That's nothing,' I told him. 'Anyone who studied well would have gotten that mark.' "

No wonder Yoel was drawn to bad friends — they didn't work on his humility! They made him feel good and gave him a generous helping of compliments without fear of kindling a spark of arrogance in him. And why *should* he invest in studying if, after all the effort, it turned out that he hadn't done anything special?

Good educators know how important it is to dish out generous helpings of encouragement and well-earned praise. They aren't afraid that it will lead to arrogance. They understand that we have neither the ability nor the obligation to make someone else — even our own son — humble. If we try to do so directly, we will only succeed in breaking him.

The truth is not arrogance, and humility cannot be founded on falsehood. Whoever has special talents is obligated to be aware of them and to make good use of them.

❖   ❖   ❖

Some people are so "humble" that they allow others to walk all over them. More on that will be presented in the coming chapter.

Assert Your Rights

"My boss is exploiting me," said Mr. Samuels. "He assigns me jobs that weren't part of our original agreement and that I don't want to do. And of all the chutzpah, he calls me at home late at night about work!"

In a free country, no one can force us to do things against our will or stop us from doing what we want. Only we ourselves can. The choice is ours; we must decide whether or not to put up with abuse.

Obviously, if you don't like how your boss is treating you, you can have a meeting to discuss your work conditions. You can make it clear, in a nice way, that you feel uncomfortable when he assigns you tasks that you haven't agreed on. If he calls you at home, you have every right to tell him that you are happy to work for him, but only in the office during work hours; you don't want to be disturbed at home, especially late at night.

Mr. Samuels didn't have the confidence to stand up to his employer. He was afraid. "I know I have the right to tell the boss to stop exploiting me," he said, "but why quarrel with him? Maybe there's a way to tolerate his behavior?"

Why, indeed, should you stand up for your rights when someone exploits you? Why not just grin and bear it for the sake of avoiding conflict?

Because you are angry, and anger is not something you should ignore. It needs to be expressed or dealt with properly. Otherwise, it won't just go away; it will go underground and attack you. If you keep quiet for fear of incurring the boss's wrath, you will turn into a frustrated person. You will seethe with resentment — against your employer for mistreating you and, worse yet, against yourself for not having the guts to stand up for your legitimate rights. The image you already have of yourself as a weakling will be reinforced, and as a result, you will become even more timid.

Suppressed anger turns into self-hate and guilt. People who allow themselves to be victimized hate themselves for being weak; they even tend to justify their attacker and blame themselves. That's why we find "good" people who never get angry — and suffer from intense fears and from painful feelings of being helpless and abnormal.

Learn how to stand up for your rights, even if it is uncomfortable at first. You'll get used to it in due time. With every brave action you take, your self-confidence will increase, your fears will decrease, and you will become more assertive.

As for the boss, he will probably respect you for speaking up and will stop exploiting you. Of course, there is always a small chance that he will threaten to fire you for your audacity. But you have the right — perhaps even the obligation — to decide not to let people walk all over you.

Exploitation is not the exclusive domain of employers. It can even be done by someone who loves you. A classic example is the mother who is anxious to see her daughter married, but has trouble letting go of her after the wedding. She may even make demands that threaten the new marriage.

> **R**achel cared devotedly for her chronically ill mother for years. After Rachel got married, the mother, playing on her guilt feelings, demanded that Rachel continue to care for her. The new husband spent every evening home alone, but Rachel "couldn't say no" to her sick mother.

Rachel should make it clear to her mother that she loves her and will do her best to care for her, but not at the expense of her marriage. If her mother tries to make her feel guilty, Rachel should respond: "I'm sorry you feel that way," and continue doing what she knows is right.

If we want to succeed and to live happy lives, we must resolve that we ourselves will determine what is right for us, in light of the halachah and in accordance with our values and principles. And we will not let anyone, no matter who he is, take advantage of us!

Don't Expect Fairness

Many people keep themselves busy crusading against injustice. They are walking encyclopedias of wrongs committed by society. In this way they guarantee themselves generous daily helpings of bitterness.

Why do they do it? Possibly it allows them to blame others for their own failures and to indulge in self-pity. Of course it would be nice if others were always honest and fair, but if they aren't, instead of fuming, we need to find ways of protecting ourselves from them.

Watch out for the trap of expecting others to be saintly! If others are guilty, and you must wait for them to change, you have given them control of your life!

It's a shame to waste one bit of energy getting angry over the dishonesty of others. Are there wicked people and swindlers in the world? There surely are. But they can't force us to collaborate with them. No one can trap us unless we give them the power to. If you choose to give in to them out of fear, go right ahead. You have the right to choose what you want to do, even if you will suffer for it. But don't complain! Is it their fault that you lack the backbone to stand up to them? As the saying goes, if you act like a donkey, don't complain about those who try to ride you. If you love the feeling of being a martyr, go right ahead being one.

If you feel exploited, evidently you don't know the rule that **no one can force you to do something against your will.**

If you're ashamed to ask the boss for a well-deserved raise, don't complain that he didn't give it to you. If someone stands on your foot on a crowded bus, you have every right to ask him to remove his foot; if you are afraid to, *you* have a problem.

The Truth Comes Out

"My roommates use me as their indentured servant," Yankie fumed. "They send me to buy them pizza, mail their letters, and even pick up their clothes from the dry cleaner. To add insult to injury, they even make fun of me for being an errand boy! It's positively humiliating."

"Why are you angry at them?" I said. "If you agree to all their requests, they would have to be fools not to take advantage of you! They also have good, though *not justified, reason for making fun of the fact that you submit willingly to exploitation!"*

I worked with Yankie on his self-confidence, so that he would understand that he has the right to refuse. Then we progressed to reacting with assertiveness.

After that, he came back with a different complaint. "I've become a bad person," he said. "I don't want to do anyone favors, and I refuse to do anything people ask of me. It's all because of you!"

"Apparently," I said, "if you do not want to do anyone favors, you were not graced with an especially good heart. You'll have to work on improving it."

The brave new approach to life that Yankie learned simply brought the truth out into the open. The solution for him was not to go on being fearful and allowing his friends to exploit him, but to improve his character and his interpersonal relations.

Mr. *Krinsky came to me with his 16-year-old son. "Nosson is unassertive," said Mr. Krinsky unhappily. "He doesn't know how to open his mouth and stand up for himself."*

After I had worked intensively with Nosson for a while, Mr. Krinsky came back to me. "You've ruined my son!"

"In what way?" I asked.

"While he was home for vacation," said Mr. Krinsky, "I woke him up at 4 in the morning to study Torah. He refused — said he was tired and wanted to sleep. In the past, he would get up without any complaints or excuses. Now he's learned from you to refuse. What good is becoming assertive if it's at the expense of Torah study?"

"If Nosson doesn't want to get up before dawn to study Torah," I explained to the startled father, "evident-

ly you haven't succeeded in educating him to do it. The fact that in the past he went along with you didn't come from love of Torah, he was simply afraid to speak up. Now you have to prove your ability to educate."

I couldn't reveal that Nosson's difficulties with assertiveness were a reaction to his father's relentless hounding. The boy used to leave the house, saying that he was going to the *beis midrash*, and then wander wherever he wished. His father had been pleased — until I mixed in and taught Nosson that instead of lying to his father and going behind his back, he should try to explain: Since he studied long, hard hours when yeshivah was in session, during vacation he wanted a break. Why shouldn't he be able to relax at home?

What I did tell Mr. Krinsky was this: "If correct education were done by suppressing a child's independence and developing a weak personality (as too many people actually think), you shouldn't teach him to walk, lest he go to forbidden places; and you shouldn't teach him to talk, lest he speak *lashon hara*. We must teach our children to be strong and self-confident, and educate them to aspire to good things. If you haven't done that, don't blame me!"

Assertiveness doesn't mean rebelling against all principles and doing whatever you desire. It means accepting principles because you freely choose to do so, not out of fear, shame, or desire to avoid unpleasantness.

What Is Assertiveness?

When someone does something that disturbs us, we can react in one of three ways: aggressively — attacking him for what he is doing; passively — suffering in silence out of fear or to avoid unpleasantness, which is what we've been discussing until now; or assertively — telling him frankly that we don't feel comfortable with what he is doing, and politely insisting on being treated properly.

Let's say the neighbor turns up the volume on his stereo late at night, and it's disturbing your sleep, Three possible reactions are:

- Aggressive: "Why don't you have some consideration for anyone else?!"
- Passive: You clench your lips and keep quiet; the neighbor might not like your interference.
- Assertive: "I have a problem sleeping when the music is loud. Would you mind turning it down?"

Each type of reaction will produce a different result. The aggressive reaction provokes strife; feeling attacked, the neighbor will probably counterattack in self-defense. The passive reaction leads to frustration, since the situation will continue until the neighbor decides on his own to turn down the volume. Both the aggressive and the passive reactions damage the relationship.

By reacting assertively, you take control of the situation without attacking the neighbor or accusing him of any wrongdoing. When you say that you are uncomfortable, he can't tell you that you aren't. Most likely he will honor your request; he would feel uneasy about ignoring it.

"I'm freezing in the dormitory," said Eli. "My roommate always turns on the air-conditioner even when I ask him not to."

"How do you ask?" I inquired.

"I say" — here Eli raised his voice — " 'In such cold weather, you turn on the air-conditioner? Are you normal?' "

I advised him to try saying graciously, "I get really cold when you turn on the air-conditioner. I would be grateful if you would take that into account."

Eli tried it. The roommate retorted, "You won't tell me what to do!" — but a minute later, he turned the air-conditioner off.

Criticism is aggressive. Whenever you get the urge to cri cize someone — in a friendship, at work, and certainly i marriage — remember:

criticism › guilt feelings › defensiveness › counterattacks

For instance, Mrs. Stein feels hurt; Mr. Stein didn't look up from his newspaper when she came home.

If she criticizes him for ignoring her, he will probably enumerate the times he did pay attention to her and conclude, "Nothing I do is ever good enough."

On the other hand, if she says, "I was very disappointed; I was expecting more attention from you," he won't feel attacked, and it will be much harder for him to ignore her hurt feelings.

Why aren't people comfortable about being assertive? Because it takes courage to tell someone that you were hurt by what he did, and it takes self-confidence to tell him your expectations. But the other alternatives — getting into a fight or suffering helplessly — are much worse.

If you learn to be assertive, you will feel that you're in control — and that will make you feel good about yourself. You will never feel like a helpless victim, nor will you attack others. You will simply stand up for your rights and respectfully demand what is rightfully coming to you.

With a little creative thought, you can use assertiveness to achieve dramatic successes in all your relationships.

I have sometimes seen a person who has not been attacked say, "I don't care how you feel. I'm going to continue doing what I'm doing!" If someone responds that way after *not* being attacked, you may want to cut off the relationship. No one has to put up with manipulation or abuse.

This is true among friends and acquaintances, but also within the family, and even between husband and wife. Friendship and domestic harmony must be based on mutual respect and consideration.

By being assertive, you can achieve a healthy relationship.

Try it. It's less scary than you think.

Think Logically

One of the most common problems of people who lack self-confidence is that they have "Divine inspiration." They read other people's minds and even foretell the future. Unfortunately, their readings and prophecies are all negative: They always see rejection, refusal, mockery, opposition, and failure.

No one in his right mind would *declare* that he has such supernatural talents. But when we don't do something because we're "sure" people will laugh at us, or when we don't ask for a raise because we "know" the boss will turn down our request, aren't we relying on our ability to read minds and predict reactions?

Of course, to a certain extent our whole thought process is built on predictions of the future. Foretelling the ramifications of our actions spells the difference between the wise and the foolish. "Who is wise? He who foresees the consequences" (*Tamid* 32a). Nevertheless, and in spite of Murphy's Law, we must be aware that **not every bad thing that can happen will happen.**

When it comes to the future, there is no such thing as realism. No forecast of future events can be more than an educated guess. It may be highly probable based on past experience, but it is possible for things to take a different turn. Turn the pages of history books, and you will see how many wise people made forecasts based on experience and understanding — and were wrong. Wars have been initiated by great commanders who were convinced that they would win — yet they lost. Prisons are full of criminals who were convinced they wouldn't be caught. People have chosen spouses, jobs, and employees, sure that it was all going to work out beautifully — and it didn't. Pictures have been painted, songs composed, books written by people who were convinced they were masterpieces — and reality proved them wrong. No ordinary person can say that his predictions always come true.

The same applies to trying to analyze and understand someone else's motives. Even the wisest professional analyst with a wealth of experience can do no more than hit the target more often than someone else. But he cannot hit it every time.

Nor can we know for certain how a person will react. The possibility that your employer *may* reject your request does not mean he *will*. And if you want to do something, but fear that So-and-so *may not* approve, remember that this doesn't mean he *won't*.

You surely have no way of knowing that *everyone* will disapprove, as those who lack confidence tend to think. If you want to move ahead, remember this truth: "It is impossible that I won't encounter any opposition. Probably some people will approve of what I do and some won't; and those who won't are bound to range from mildly disapproving to out-and-out opposing."

Actually, self-confident people don't generally delve deeply into the subject of what *X* will say and how *Y* will react. Those who lack self-confidence are more inclined to worry about it. Some know that the results they dread are unlikely to happen, but they aren't willing to take even a slight risk. Many assume that whatever can happen will, and their belief that the worst-case scenario will happen paralyzes them.

Yisrael had problems finding a chavrusa in yeshivah. Actually, he hadn't even tried to look for one because "it's obvious that no one will want to learn with me."

"If you ask five boys to learn with you," I said, "how many do you think will refuse?"

"All of them."

"Do you know, *or do you* think *that's what will happen?"*

"I'm firmly convinced of it."

"There's no point in arguing over what will happen in the future," I said. "I can't prove to you that you'll find a chavrusa if only you will try, and you can't prove to me that nothing will help.

"But you know what?" I challenged him. "I propose that you prove to me once and for all that you're right! Make an experiment and ask five boys if they will learn with you. Record their answers. If they all turn you down, I admit defeat."

Yisrael left my house grinning as if to say, "I'll show him!"

A day later, he returned. He was totally amazed. Out of the five he had approached, five had responded positively!

Now he had a new problem: which of the five to choose.

No, I'm not a prophet. I didn't know which boys he would approach, much less what answers they would give. But I was sure of one thing: The possibility that they *might* say "no" did not mean that they *would*.

We never know how someone will react until he does. By giving in to our apprehension and accepting the assumption that we will be turned down, we deny ourselves the possibility of ever succeeding.

Logical Versus Emotional Thinking

Learn to differentiate between logical and emotional thinking. By emotional thinking I mean arriving at a conclusion because of a feeling; in logical thinking, you can explain how you got there and what facts you used.

Intuition is a wonderful tool. It's great for pointing out which direction we should look into, or guiding us after we have the facts and can't decide between various options. But keep things in proportion. You still need solid facts to come to a wise decision. Relying on a vague feeling as if it were absolute truth is liable to cause you bitter mistakes.

Moreover, only when you present an argument based on facts can the truth be tested. There is no convincing a person who "has a feeling." Concrete evidence to the contrary won't help him see the light. He won't even be able to convince himself.

M rs. Summers "had a feeling" that she was critically ill. She spent most of her time preparing her will and other necessities for leaving this world.

No medical tests could convince Mrs. Summers that she was healthy. Neither could the fact that she lived a long life and attended the funerals of two friends who had laughed at her.

Feelings can be misleading. Can't you recall times when you were "sure" beyond the shadow of a doubt, and later turned out to be wrong?

People who lack self-confidence tend to rely on emotional thinking, blindly regarding past, present, and future. Instead of thoroughly checking the facts, they read minds and prophecy. Sometimes things get to the point of the absurd. And mind you, I'm talking about people who are normal.

***M**r. Stoll is a highly respected lawyer. No one is aware of his acute feelings of inferiority. One day he went for a medical checkup to find out why he was suffering from stomach aches. The doctor told him that his muscles were tense; he should relax a little.*

"I feel hurt," he told me, "because the doctor thinks I'm just complaining, and it's nothing more than a case of nerves."

"Is that what he said to you?"

"No; he didn't want to insult me. But maybe you can tell me why he thinks that way?"

If you don't understand how Mr. Stoll arrived at his conclusion, that's okay. I also had to hear the story two or three times before I caught on. And don't forget that we're talking about a regular fellow, the kind who might be sitting beside you in shul, and you would never imagine what he thinks you think of him.

Don't laugh at such people. All of us make absurd misappraisals in some measure or other. But we forgive ourselves.

That's how the world is. Everyone understands his own foibles, but thinks someone else's are ridiculous.

I am sure that a mighty burst of laughter would echo across the world if we knew, even for just one minute, what foibles and fears others have. On second thought, it might bring relief to all of us, for we could then say, "What I have isn't so terrible. Everyone is like that."

Everyone *is* like that. I've discovered this after counseling hundreds of people who are completely normal. We're all slightly different versions of the same book.

Predict
a Rosy Future

Although normal people cannot predict the future, they *can* influence it through their predictions.

Reuven and Shimon are about to be interviewed by the manager of a company. Their resumes indicate that the two are equally qualified for the job, but the manager can hire only one.

Reuven enters the room with erect posture and a confident smile on his face. He looks the manager in the eye, gives him a firm handshake, and says, "Good morning." The manager is favorably impressed even before he begins the interview. Shimon goes in with a worried face and hesitant steps, timidly extends the tips of his fingers, and mumbles, "Good morning," so quietly that the manager must ask him to repeat what he said.

Which man do you think the manager will hire? Why should the company think Shimon will succeed if Shimon doesn't think he will? Wouldn't it make sense for the manager to prefer Reuven, who looks like someone who knows what he's doing, can shoulder a heavy burden, and will get the job done?

What was and what will be do not exist. The only thing that exists in reality is this minute — the present. When Reuven and Shimon approach a challenge, both see the future in their imagination. Reuven sees it in rosy hues; Shimon sees it in shades of gray and black. Both rely on their "prophecy." And these prophecies are self-fulfilling. Reuven's prediction that he would succeed at the interview caused him to succeed; Shimon's prediction that he would fail made him fail.

There isn't any hocus-pocus about self-fulfilling prophecy. Visualizing yourself succeeding allows you to throw yourself into a project with all your energy, which naturally boosts your chances of success. Someone who foresees himself failing trips himself up. Why should he try hard if his work will go down the drain anyway? With such thinking, even if he has the ability to reach his goals, he won't get there.

John is able to lift a 100-pound weight, and he knows that this is the limit of his ability. Mark gives him a weight that is marked "100," but that he somehow made a few pounds heavier. "Knowing" that he can pick it up, John musters all his strength and manages to lift it. Then Mark gives him a 100-pound weight that is marked "120." Chances are that he won't be able to pick it up, because since he is convinced that he can't do it, he won't make much of an effort.

If you are still skeptical about self-fulfilling prophecies, or the power of suggestion, just think of the placebo effect, where a sick person given a sugar pill recovers because he believes he has taken effective medicine. Think of the advertisement industry, which capitalizes on the power of suggestion and spends billions tricking us all into "needing" what they want us to buy.

We're not speaking here about people of low intelligence. Research shows that everyone is susceptible to suggestion. So use it to increase your self-confidence — and your effectiveness will soar.

A voice teacher told me that when a group of people sing together, each of them is able to reach higher tones than if he sang alone.

"Why?" I asked.

"When one person sings alone," the voice teacher explained, "he hesitates to try a high tone for fear that he won't reach it. Since he doesn't try hard enough, of course he fails. But in a group, he has no fear of failure, since even if it happens it will go unnoticed. With the fear gone, he produces more."

Thus our predictions about ourselves translate into belief or lack of belief in our ability. The one breeds success; the other, failure. The degree of success depends directly on the measure of faith in our ability.

The managers of a major corporation wanted to stimulate their engineers to be more creative. They brought in a team of professional advisers to investigate what distinguishes an engineer who is creative from one who is not.

After questioning the engineers in detail and studying the situation for three months, the advisers presented their startling results. One factor made all the difference: The engineers who were creative believed that they were creative, and the less creative ones believed that they were less creative.

A person is what he believes he is. Your ability is the result of your belief in it.

I'm not saying that faith alone can change reality in every instance. I wouldn't expect you to move a wall with your bare hands simply because you believe in your ability to move it. But faith does work wonders in magnifying your chances of success in things that you can naturally do.

Let's say we rate a particular difficulty as 5 on a scale of 0 to 10, where 0 is the easiest and 10 the hardest. Confidence in your ability to overcome the difficulty will change its rating to 4, 3, or perhaps even 2. Doubt in your ability to overcome it will raise the degree of difficulty a few points.

The past is over and done with, but the future is in our hands. Of course, we need G-d's help first and foremost. But, as we have seen, G-d usually helps a person through natural means, and success naturally needs faith in our ability as its starting point. If we believe we can succeed, we will.

G risha Stein left Russia at the age of 50 and settled in a small town in Israel. To support his family, he opened a sandwich stand near the main road.

Grisha was hard of hearing, so he didn't listen to the radio. He had difficulty seeing, so he didn't read the newspapers. But he knew how to make delicious sandwiches. He applied to the municipality and received permission to put up signs advertising his delicious sandwiches at the side of the main road.

People saw the signs, and they stopped and bought. Month by month his sales increased. He expanded his stand, bought a bigger oven and an extra refrigerator, and ordered larger quantities of rolls and other groceries. His business thrived.

One day Grisha's brother, a man of the world, came to visit. When he saw the efforts Grisha was putting into expanding his business, he remarked, "Haven't you read in the papers that the country is in recession? Didn't you hear on the radio that the Middle East is on the brink of war? Don't you know that there's a crisis in the stock market and people have lost millions?"

Grisha thought to himself, Well, he reads the papers and listens to the radio. He must know what's going on. How lucky I am to have a brother who warns me in time!

So Grisha went and took down his signs from the side of the road, sold his big oven and refrigerator, cut down his orders, and prepared fewer sandwiches. Almost overnight, his sales began to go down. Each day, they sank more and more.

"You were right," Grisha told his knowing brother. "There is definitely a terrible recession."

Decide and Do

e have seen that in order to do anything, we need the will to do it and the confidence that we can succeed at it. But even when we have both, we may still hesitate for fear of making the wrong decision.

Of course it is wise to consider the consequences and weigh all the pros and cons before making a decision. But weigh each matter in proportion to its importance. Then decide and carry out your decision. Remember that your analysis is only a means, not an end.

Some people treat the deliberations as if they were a goal. They spend so much time and mental energy in thinking about what to do and how to do it, and they are so full of doubt, that they get stuck in the planning stage and don't move on to action. Their real problem is that they don't believe they have the wisdom to make the right decision.

If you need any information about kitchen tables, call Mrs. Smith; she's a walking encyclopedia on the subject. How did that happen? Mrs. Smith needed a new kitchen table. She made lists of all the models of tables, where they can be bought and for what price, what materials they are made of, and how they are finished. She found out which of her friends bought which table, what each purchaser thinks of her table, and who got the best payment terms.

So how does Mrs. Smith like her new table? Well, she doesn't have one yet. She is drowning in the sea of information and can't decide which table to choose.

You see chronic hesitaters in the local grocery store. They're the ones who stand beside a shelf, deliberating over which can of peas to buy. They think through every trivial decision as if their lives depended on it. If they would once stop to calculate how much time they waste on their deliberations, they would be astounded to discover how many hours they invest in this process, not to mention the emotional energy.

But that's nothing compared to what happens afterward. They are never satisfied with what they chose. They mull over how much better it would have been had they chosen differently, and eat themselves up over their decision, which was "wrong, as usual."

The Cause

Chronic hesitation can come either from negative past experiences or from lack of practice in decision-making.

A chronic hesitater may have been burned long ago when he made a poor decision, and his parents or teachers put him down. Instead of teaching him how to weigh the options and decide more wisely in the future, they "taught" him that he doesn't have what it takes to make decisions. Ever since, he's been playing it safe. Fearful of making a wrong decision, he tells others that he can't decide and asks for help. That way, no one will be able to blame him for any untoward results.

Another type of chronic hesitater was never given the opportunity to make his own decisions. As a child, everything was decided for him: which cereal to eat for breakfast, which shirt to put on, which friends to invite home, and which games to play. His parents constantly bombarded him with wise advice in the hope of sparing him from making the same mistakes they had made. They forgot that their wisdom came to them only *thanks* to their own mistakes.

Both those who were burned and those whose parents prevented them from suffering the "burns" so vital for developing independence are afraid to make their own decisions. Long after reaching adulthood, they search with candles for "advisers" who will help them make decisions about everything in their lives — like the girls who, after they get married, call Mom every day to ask what to cook for supper.

Regardless of the causes, anyone can learn how to make better and faster decisions.

The Problem and Its Solution

Why is decision-making so hard?

Imagine yourself standing before a fork in the road. Now you have two options. But once you decide, you are not only choosing one road. You are also rejecting the other!

Before you make any decision, all your options are open. You feel free and in control. Once you decide, you lose these enjoyable sensations. What's more, you close the door on the other opportunity. And in your heart you may harbor the thought that perhaps you made a mistake, and the option you rejected was the better of the two.

Let's say you want to buy a new house in a certain neighborhood. There are two houses for sale within your budget; both are in excellent condition, and the price for both is the same. One house has an extra bedroom, but the other has a large garden. You would love to have both advantages. Should you choose the extra bedroom or the garden? It's not hard to take one; the difficulty is giving up the other.

If so, how can we ever decide?

Part of being careful is not to be *too* careful (*Chovos HaLevavos*).

That is, be careful not to overdo caution by using it where it isn't needed (*Pas Lechem*). Always think before you act — but the amount of thinking you do should be commensurate with the importance of the decision.

When the decision involves choosing a spouse, a new house, or a yeshivah in which to learn, by all means consult the specialists. Check every aspect in detail; leave no stone unturned in your investigations. Try not to leave room for mistakes, because any mistake you make will be very costly. But why invest a great deal of energy and thought in small decisions?

A cold sweat covered Mr. Rabinowitz's face and his forehead was wrinkled from tense thought. To see him deliberate over whether to pray in the first or second minyan, you would think he was the president deciding whether to declare war on a foreign country.

It was very sad. His life had turned into a heavy burden. By noon he was often exhausted as if he had a long, hard day of work behind him. His suffering was as great as it was needless.

What will happen if you don't make the right decision? Will they hang you at the city gates? Will the world come to an end?

Besides, who says there *is* one right decision? If you had to choose between an excellent option and a poor one, it would be understandable that you find the choice a weighty responsibility. The irony is that in such a case, you would decide quickly! No one hesitates over whether he should exit his fourth-floor apartment through the door or through the window, or whether to put good milk or sour milk into his coffee. Hesitation appears when the choice is between good options, with strong points in favor of each. In such a case, what harm can come of your choice, whatever it is?

I asked Mr. Rabinowitz to make an experiment. Whenever he had difficulty choosing between two options, he would deliberately choose the worse one. He would record both options and his final decision in a notebook.

Two weeks later, we examined his notebook together to see what harm had befallen him for choosing the worse option. Not only had no catastrophe occurred — in many cases, precisely the option that had looked worse turned out to be the better one.

I know a businessman who has to clinch many big deals daily. If he were to hesitate over every proposal, he wouldn't have time left to make any deals at all. In order to overcome his hesitation, he hung the following sign on the wall facing his desk: **I, too, am allowed to make mistakes.**

How much wisdom and decision-making talent lies behind this slogan!

It's perfectly normal to make mistakes; everyone does. Whenever you do, be happy — you've learned what not to do next time! Life is one long learning process, and you can't do things right if you don't make mistakes.

Even if you don't make the very best choice, life won't come to an end. You will have plenty of opportunities to make better choices. And we must learn to live well also with a choice that's second best.

Don't be afraid of mistakes. There's something much worse than a bad decision: **the decision not to decide.**

An Exercise

If you suffer from excessive hesitation, I recommend an exercise for learning how to decide quickly and well. (This exercise does not apply to truly fateful decisions; there it is wise to consult a sage.) For one week:

- Don't ask anyone for advice. No matter how difficult it is, decide yourself and be willing to pay the price of erring.
- Place a time limit on deliberations. After that, even if you haven't reached a conclusion, choose one option or the other without further deliberation.

After a week, evaluate your decision-making. You will probably find that the price of error was not so high. Perhaps you could have made a better decision, but you certainly did not make the worst decision possible, and no one can do more than that. Repeat the exercise the following week, and then the week after that. Little by little, you will learn to make decisions without fear of mistakes. And **the less afraid you are of mistakes, the less chance you have of making them.**

Hesitation in Spiritual Matters

Many people have some degree of doubt as to whether they are serving G-d properly. Most of them are youths with a strong conscience and a high ethical level. While we definitely should make sure that all our actions are in line with the Creator's will, we have to be careful not to torment ourselves.

In extreme cases, a young yeshivah student who ardently desires to serve G-d will agonize over every step he wants to take until the unbearable doubt saps his strength and paralyzes him.

"Going to the bookcase to choose a mussar work to study has turned into a nightmare," Menashe confided. "After I pick out one and begin to study it, doubt sets in. A voice inside tells me it would be better to learn from a different book. It gets to the point where I change books five or six times in one day."

In any aspect of serving G-d, Menashe is never sure he is doing the right thing. He has investigated various ways of Divine service but can't decide which path to choose for fear that the other option might be better. Once he wanted to be a great masmid, cut off from all his surroundings and devoted solely to Torah study, and once a gomel chesed who takes care of everyone in need. He examines himself ceaselessly, and goes around with the constant feeling that he is missing something. No matter what he does, his heart tells him he should be doing something else.

The feeling of always being at the crossroads and not knowing which way to go stems from a fundamental error. People think that there is only one way to serve G-d as an observant Jew — and if one way is correct, the other path must be false. So they go out and search for the one and only true path to follow.

But there is no one true path to follow! The *Arizal* said that there were twelve gates to heaven, and each of the twelve tribes served its Creator through the gate that was appropriate to it (*Shaar HaKavanos*). You can become righteous whether you are a *chassid* or a *misnaged*, you can become a Torah scholar in any yeshivah, and you can learn character improvement from any *mussar* work. "These and those are the words of the Living G-d" (*Eruvin* 13b). There are many ways to climb the spiritual ladder, and **you have the right to choose the way closest to your heart** and best suited to your personality.

Please Yourself [1]

Before the freezer was invented, Frederic Tudor visited the West Indies. Sweltering in the heat, he thought longingly of the ice on his father's pond in Massachusetts, and wished he had some to cool his drink.

He returned to Massachusetts with a new idea: He would ship ice to hot countries for iced drinks. Everyone laughed at him. Sell ice? What could be sillier? And how could he keep it from melting?

Tudor didn't care what they thought of him. He worked on his idea, found that sawdust can protect ice from heat, built special houses in hot countries to hold the ice, and bought the rights to cut ice from all the ponds in his area. Let them

1. Our discussion does not apply to matters prohibited by halachah or our rabbinic leaders.

laugh. By 1850, he had made a fortune shipping over 150,000 tons of ice to nearly every hot country in the world.

Tudor wasn't plagued by the question, "What will they think of me?"

On the other hand, we can't totally ignore the question. We have to walk the fine line between consideration for others and total self-denial. The need for approval is natural, legitimate, and good. Healthy adaptation to our social environment shows fine character, as our Sages taught: "If people are pleased with someone, G-d is pleased with him" (*Avos* 3:13).

G-d created man with a need to live in society and to be accepted by it. A central part of the Torah deals with the social aspect of life. Many of the positive commandments and prohibitions teach us how to relate to those around us and live in harmony with society. R' Akiva said, " 'Love your neighbor as yourself; I am Hashem' (*Vayikra* 19:18) is a great principle of the Torah" (*Yerushalmi, Nedarim* 9:4). When a gentile asked Hillel to convert him "on condition that you teach me the whole Torah while I stand on one foot," Hillel told him, "That which is hateful to you, do not do to others. This is the whole Torah; the rest is explanation. Go learn it" (*Shabbos* 31a).

It's essential to develop friendly, close relationships with other people. We must give to them and take from them to satisfy our physical and emotional needs. Someone who goes off to live alone in the wilderness has a slim chance for survival; we need others even for minimum food, clothing, and shelter. But we also need their esteem, and we need to feel that we make a difference to someone in the world. To satisfy these needs, we must take a sincere interest in others — and then they will reciprocate, for "as water reflects a face back to a face, so one's heart is reflected back to him by another" (*Mishlei* 27:19).

Men build on the experience of their predecessors. Most "new" inventions are refinements and modifications of older ones. The ancient Egyptians' sundials were based on the

Babylonians' shadow-and-pole arrangement for measuring the passing of time. Henry Ford's assembly-line production was based on methods used by other companies. Louis Braille's alphabet of raised dots was inspired by Charles Barbier's system of embossing coded dot-and-dash messages on cardboard. The Wright brothers' plane was preceded by the planes of de la Croix and of Ader. Alexander Graham Bell's telephone wasn't much use until Thomas Edison's variable-contact carbon transmitter increased the power of its electrical signals.

Spiritually, too, we can derive tremendous benefit from the wisdom and experience of others. *R' Moshe Chaim Luzzatto* explained with an analogy:

> **P**rinces would plant a garden maze for amusement. The objective was to reach a gazebo in the center. To get there, you had to choose from among many winding paths, most of which led further away from the gazebo. You had no way of knowing whether you had chosen the right path — but the person who had already reached the gazebo knew, for he saw the paths before him. Similarly, those who are struggling with their evil inclination cannot be certain if they are keeping to the right path — but the person who has already mastered his evil inclination can advise others how to do it (Mesillas Yesharim, Ch. 3).

We need others as a grinding stone on which to sharpen our minds. Debating leads to discovery of the truth. Research has shown that yeshivah students have an above-average ability for logical analysis because they study in pairs. The *Rambam* explains why it is that, if *all* the Sanhedrin's judges agree that a person being tried is guilty of a capital offense, he goes free: Human reason is easily mistaken, and only an opinion formed after hearing a conflicting view can yield the truth (*Moreh*

Nevuchim, cited in *Divrei Shaul, Vayeira*). We need to cooperate closely with others in order to achieve wisdom.

So we must take others' viewpoints into account, be sincerely courteous, and not belittle them. We must not make ourselves so conspicuous that we stick out like a sore thumb.

If you belong to a group, don't be a wise guy. A cohesive community offers its members many benefits; at the same time, it demands a certain degree of conformity and has every right to do so. If you want to live within such a framework, you must abide by its conventions. If you don't like the conventions, you have the right to leave — but don't try to have your cake and eat it too. You can't both live within it and rebel against it. Not only would that be disrespectful and incorrect, it also creates psychological problems for the nonconformists and their children. So if you're a Belzer *chassid* like me, make sure to behave according to Belz standards; and if you're studying in a white-shirt, dark-suit yeshivah, don't walk around in sport shirt and blue jeans.

The Other Side of the Coin

Part of living in a community is knowing your place and balancing your personal reality against the image you want to project. Every community has its VIPs and rank and file, its rabbis and laymen, its wealthy and poor. Each one of these groups has a different mode of behavior. A lavish wedding that a wealthy person makes for his only daughter will not seem necessary, or justified, to someone on a lower economic level.

What type of bar mitzvah should *I* make — a lavish feast like X made, or one that is appropriate to my own pocketbook? Should the family dress like the rich or make do with affordable clothes? Someone once observed that people spend money that they don't have to buy what they don't need to impress people whom they don't like. And some women buy a fur coat not so that they will be warm, but so that their neighbor will be cold.

How can you tell whether you did something because you really wanted to or because of social duress?

We can fool ourselves with false reasoning, but we can't fool our feelings. These accurate sensors of the soul reveal the truth. So after the fact, examine your feelings. If you acceded to the wish of others because you saw the good in it, you will be happy. But if you did so out of fear, you will feel frustrated, resentful, and humiliated.

You don't even have to wait till after the fact — you can use your imagination to figure out how you will feel afterwards.

If we sacrifice all our desires and needs for others and are afraid to voice any opinion that is unacceptable to them, we are headed for disaster. A person who is totally dependent on the approval of others suffers in many ways.

He is always nervous about whether he has managed to please everyone. But although he bends over backwards, he never succeeds.

He surrenders control of his happiness to others. If they support him, he feels comfortable; if they express a contrary opinion, he is miserable. He is plagued by hesitation lest he make a decision of which they won't approve. The constant fear of what they will say robs him of peace of mind and drains his physical and emotional energy.

To make matters even worse, exploiters are drawn to him like sharks to blood. They have a field day manipulating him. If he steps out of line, they need only throw out a comment like "How could you do such a thing? I wouldn't have expected this from *you*." Overwhelmed by guilt as if he had committed a war crime, he will quickly do an about-face to avoid another such accusation. But his heart will ache over the great sacrifice he has made for them. For he has handed over his independence on a silver platter, and instead of appreciating it, they despise him for it. Anger and resentment build up inside him against society in general. "They" are not fair; they show no consideration for his opinions or wishes; they run his whole life and decide everything for him! If only he could rise up and rebel against them! But since he is too timid to do so, he will escape his pain by fantasizing about how much better his lot would be "if *they* were different."

We have to know where to set the limits so that we don't let the fear of "What will *they* say?" rule our lives.

How Did It Happen?

How do people become excessively dependent on the approval of others?

Early on in life, we were taught to consider what others are thinking. Parents and teachers reacted with approval or disapproval to anything we did or said. Gradually we learned to think before taking action; not, *Is this action wise and good?* but, *What will* they *say?* As this habit was reinforced throughout our school years, it became second nature. We had to walk the narrow path that our educators set for us, and we were punished for every deviation.

This is not to say that we *always* stayed in line. Sometimes the urge to say or do something unusual welled up within us. Then, if our mistake evoked a harsh reaction, we became even more fearful of ever again doing something that wouldn't please them.

When this occurs repeatedly, a weak person may conclude that his own opinion is worthless. He will feel inferior, lack backbone, and always seek the approval of others.

Sounds extreme? Just between you and me, we all suffer from this syndrome to some extent.

Inner Doubt

If we look a little deeper, we will see that our need for approval stems from inner doubt. Someone who feels confident that he is right will not worry about what others will say.

Take Leah, who is down in the dumps because she thinks that her friends think she's stupid. If Leah thought she was smart, it wouldn't occur to her that others think she isn't. If she were convinced beyond a shadow of a doubt that she is smart even if people told her bluntly that she was stupid, she wouldn't believe them. (Try telling a fool convinced of his own brilliance that he's stupid!) When will such a remark disturb her? Only if a doubt about her intelligence has already stolen into her heart.

If you have ten fingers, and someone comes over and tells you that you have only nine, you'll laugh at him. If you're walking down the street and a stranger shouts at you, "Murderer! Why did you kill my father?" you'll think he's crazy and look at him with pity.

If someone makes fun of your black hair, you won't take offense, because you're confident that there is nothing wrong with having black hair.

If you go around worrying that others might have negative thoughts about you, it's because subconsciously you have the very same negative thoughts about yourself! Projecting these negative thoughts on others is an attempt to ward off your fear that they might be true. The thought, *I'm stupid,* is scary; *If I speak up they might think I'm stupid (even if I know I'm not)* is more bearable. People with low self-esteem seem to be frightened of what others might think of them, but actually they're terrified that they *themselves* might think they're wrong. For this reason, it won't help to tell them they're okay; since they themselves believe they're not, they'll think you're just trying to console them.

That's the irony. A person who is full of self-doubt worries about what others will say, needs proof from them that he's okay, and seeks more and more encouragement — but no amount of "their" reassurance will soothe him! His doubts are inner, and not connected at all to what others say.

Sixteen-year-old Gershon would often cover his face when he smiled. After many sessions, he *told me, "When I was 12, a friend said that when I smile, my nostrils flare out in a funny way."*

Ever since then, Gershon had believed that he looks strange.

I was surprised. "You and I have spent many hours together, Gershon," I said. "I've seen you smile without covering your face, and I didn't notice anything strange."

I suggested that he check it out for himself. "Go smile at people without covering your face," I said, "and see what happens."

A week later Gershon reported that he had stopped covering his face.

In his heart, Gershon feared that he looked strange, although in truth he didn't. He was in conflict with himself, with his own fears, but ascribed the opinions about his strangeness to others.

Zevulun never stepped out of the house unless his clothes were immaculately clean and pressed and his shoes freshly shined. His appearance was perfect — too perfect. He explained to me that he did it "so that they won't think I'm a slob."

"By the way," I said, "have you seen Mr. Bullman lately?"

"Sure, I ran into him only this morning. Why do you ask?"

"Were his shoes polished? Were there any stains on his jacket?"

Zevulun raised his eyebrows and didn't answer.

After I had tossed out a few more questions of that nature, Zevulun asked in amazement, "Would any normal person pay attention to such trivial things?"

"Then why are you afraid to walk out of the house in shoes that aren't polished?"

Zevulun got the message. But it was important to understand what had happened to him. During our sessions we discovered that when he was a child, other children had teased him for being sloppy and dirty. When he got a little bigger, he decided to take himself in hand. He didn't know the limits and constantly struggled to prove "to them" that he was not a slob. This habit became so ingrained that it persisted long after "they" were no longer part of his life.

Early on, although Zevulun achieved his goal — to change their opinion about him — he never reevaluated his own opinion about his personal neatness. He was putting enormous effort into something with no benefit, since he had long ago reached his first goal.

What happened to Zevulun happens to all of us on some level. We continue trying to prove to ourselves or to others what we already succeeded in proving long ago. We are influenced by opinions about ourselves that we developed in early childhood but repressed because they were uncomfortable; thus we don't reevaluate them. In therapy for low self-esteem, we examine why we think the way we do, reevaluate the underlying assumptions, and give them a healthier, truer meaning.

Approve of Yourself!

Yes, we must be considerate of others, and naturally we want them to like us; but we must beware of sacrificing our independence and individuality on this altar.

Ask yourself:

- Does the attempt to always flow with the current, to express opinions similar to everybody else's, truly save me from being hurt by them?
- Do they respect me any more for it?

Think of people whom you truly admire. Most likely they are the ones who express their own original opinions confidently and fearlessly.

Remember that nobody has to think the way you do, and you don't have to think the way they do. If you get angry at others, it's because their behavior doesn't fit in with your desires or expectations; you assume that *they* should do what *you* think they should — which is patently absurd. And just as no one has to see reality as you see it or to think and feel as you think and feel, it is perfectly legitimate for *you* to think, feel, and see reality differently than others! No one has a monopoly on seeing the truth or on understanding fairness and justice. Everyone may act according to what is correct from his own perspective. Both sides may be right; it's a matter of different perspectives on the same reality.

Yes, we ask in Grace After Meals: "May we find favor and good understanding in the eyes of G-d and man." But we, too, fall into the category of "man." For the sake of developing our personality and increasing our self-confidence, we must also find favor in our own eyes.

We have every right to hold independent views, express ourselves, and behave as we see fit, as long as it does not harm others or violate the Torah and the instructions of our spiritual leaders. After all, each of us has to live with himself twenty-four hours a day, every day of his life.

Ask yourself:

- Why should I feel bad so that others might possibly feel good?
- Why is their opinion more important than mine?
- Why is it better to find favor in their eyes than in my own?
- Why should I please them instead of pleasing myself?
- Why should I give up my basic rights for those who don't consider my rights legitimate?

Stop trying to impress others and satisfy their demands. It won't help you. No matter what you do, there will always be someone out there who will oppose you. From the day the world was created, there was never a man whom everyone liked. Even Moshe Rabbeinu had opponents. If you try to satisfy everyone, you won't be able to satisfy anyone!

The safest way to escape all criticism is not to think, speak, or do anything. Are you prepared for that? If not, any time unjustified criticism is hurled your way, repeat to yourself:

Just as you have a right not to agree with my opinion, I have a right not to agree with yours!

If you are hit by a comment like "I wouldn't have expected that of you," try answering as I once did: "The fact that you were so wrong about me shows that you still have much to learn."

Try it, and enjoy!

Exercises

Doubting whether to do what pleases you or what impresses others is a habit, and as we've seen, habits can be overcome.

Go slowly. Don't get up one morning and declare, "From now on, I will do only what I think is right regardless of what others say." Take one step at a time.

Let's say you want to paint the inside of your house. You would be happy with a double coat of plain white paint, and that's all you can comfortably afford. But everyone else uses patterned wallpaper, which costs much more. You are assailed by doubts.

Be decisive and overcome your fears. Tell yourself, *Let* them *do with their houses and their money as* they *wish. In my house, I'll do what I like.*

When *they* asked a millionaire, "Why don't you paint the front of your house? It looks so dilapidated!" he replied, "If I wanted to spend the money, first I would paint the fronts of the houses that face mine. That's what *I* see from my living room!"

After you paint your house white, sit back and wait to see what happens. With time, having seen that nothing untoward occurs, you will acquire the courage to take a bold step in another area of your life. Little by little, the new habit will become second nature, and you will be more self-confident.

And many of *them* will envy your newfound courage and independent spirit!

*E*arly in the morning one fine spring day, an old villager and his young grandson washed and cleaned their donkey. Then, with the donkey between them, they set out on the road to the big city, to sell their donkey in the market. After walking for a while, they passed a group of people. One of them said, "Look at those fools! Instead of riding their donkey, they're walking on foot!"

The old villager heard the comment. He picked up his cap and scratched his head in amazement. "How come I didn't think of that before?" He scooped up the child and put him on the donkey. Then he got on, too, and they continued comfortably on their way.

A little while later, they met another group. The old villager was insulted to hear one of the group saying loudly, "Look at those cruel lazybones, breaking the donkey's back like that!"

"He's right," said the old villager. Since he was the heavier of the two, he jumped off the donkey and started walking on foot, while the child continued to ride the donkey. Before he had time to recover from his grave mistake, he heard people whispering, "Look at that disrespectful child, riding the donkey while that old man has to walk!"

"Hm, they're really right, aren't they?" The old villager swiftly took down the child, set him on his feet, and took his place on the donkey's back. Of course, it wasn't long before he heard, "What a despicable man. He rides comfortably on the donkey, and doesn't give a hoot about a tender child!"

Confused and exhausted, the old villager and his grandson sat down to rest at the side of the road, but *not before hearing a comment from passersby that the donkey would get exhausted from the long road to the city, and no one would want to buy it.*

The old villager and his grandson did some thinking. When they had finished resting, they got up and continued on their way, but in an entirely different manner. In the big city, the sun was setting and peddlers in the marketplace were closing their booths. Suddenly, the startled peddlers stood still and stared in disbelief. An old man and a young child, carrying a long wooden beam on their shoulders, were trudging wearily into the marketplace. In the middle of the beam, tied by its feet, hung an upside-down donkey.

Now is everybody happy?

Make Criticism Work for You

Once you are able to take decisive action without worrying about what "they" will say, you can go a step further: If they offer you constructive criticism, take it and use it!

Avoid criticism like poison — when you're on the giving end. Dispense praise generously; nothing encourages and lifts spirits like a sincere compliment.

But when you're on the receiving end, do an about-face.

Everyone makes mistakes, and we need criticism to save ourselves from additional ones. Criticism is a valuable tool for self-improvement.

Repeat to yourself over and over: **Criticism is my best friend**.

Ignore the speaker's possible motives, and focus instead on the content. Is there any truth in it? If the answer is yes, go fix what needs fixing.

"Don't rebuke a scoffer, lest he hate you," said King Solomon. "Rebuke a wise man, and he will love you" (*Mishlei* 9:8). Why? The wise man, in his desire to improve, is willing to learn from anyone. But the scoffer thinks that whatever he does is right (*Metzudas David*). In fact, that's how he became a scoffer. Since he always thought he was right, he began to scoff at everyone else's opinions (*Rabbeinu Yonah*). "Have you seen a man who is wise in his own eyes? There is more hope for a fool than for him" (*Mishlei* 26:12).

In addition to remaining with all his shortcomings, a person who rejects criticism will lack close friends. If he has no regard for their opinions, and they can't complain when he does something that hurts them, they'll keep a safe distance away. "Rebuke leads to peace," said Reish Lakish. For only after Avraham complained to Avimelech about the well that Avimelech's servants had seized did Avraham and Avimelech make a covenant (*Bereishis* 21:22–31; *Bereishis Rabbah* 54:3). If hatred flares up between people, they won't be able to make enduring peace until after explicit rebuke removes the animosity from their hearts (*Etz Yosef*).

There's no limit to the wisdom or virtues that you can acquire. If you want to succeed, you will use all possible means to reach the highest level you can. And rebuke — or criticism — is the most readily available.

Don't Be Afraid

Fear of criticism is a sign of weakness. A self-confident person is not afraid to admit he made a mistake; his self-esteem remains solid enough that he can live with it. But a person who is insecure can't admit his mistake because that would erode his shaky self-confidence even more. To shield himself from criticism, he will adopt one of several approaches.

He may set out to prove to himself and to others that he's strong. He will develop feelings of superiority and try to show how successful and smart he is. If he suspects that others are trying to criticize him, he will attack viciously to make sure they won't dare do it again.

But he can't prevent them from speaking against him behind his back. He merely prevents them from criticizing him to his face — and that's a terrible loss. It virtually guarantees that he'll repeat his mistakes. Worse yet, in the course of time he'll cut himself off from the people around him. Since he has no way of knowing what they think, his decisions won't take into account the opinions and feelings of the public he serves, the employees he manages, the colleagues he works with, or the family members he lives with. This guarantees him more and more unpleasant run-ins and humiliating failures until he finds himself detested by all.

Alternatively, a person who fears criticism may decide to keep a low profile. He will steer clear of situations in which he might be exposed to criticism. He will avoid positions of responsibility and seek work on a lower level, which draws less fire. Thus he forfeits every possible opportunity to succeed, for opportunity entails risk. He also loses a vital tool — criticism — that could have helped him become more effective.

Such a person doesn't make enemies, but he does miss out on many opportunities in the course of his life. How much talent has gone down the drain only because its owners were afraid to take responsibility!

Some insecure people use a third approach: Outwardly they reject criticism, but secretly they take it to heart. At least they use the criticism to their benefit — but they lose the critic.

> **R**euven remarked to Shimon that his behavior at a social gathering was not respectable enough. "We live in a democratic society," Shimon retorted, "and I don't need your consent!"

Despite his retort, Shimon made a mental note to try to behave better the next time. Reuven, too, made a mental note: to never again point out Shimon's mistakes.

Learn to Accept Criticism

Mistakes are inevitable. A wise person tries to minimize his losses by recognizing his mistakes and fixing them. So if you want to be effective and make the most of yourself, develop an affinity for criticism. Actively seek it. The more of it you can get, the better. Criticism is worth more than gold; "a friend who privately points out your shortcomings is better than one who gives you a gold piece every time he meets you" (*Mivchar HaPeninim, Shaar Tochechas Ahavah*). Invite criticism and encourage critics!

Be practical. Set aside your honor. As the *Rambam* said, **"Accept the truth from whoever says it"** (Introduction, *Commentary on Avos*). Separate the critic's motive — which is what usually arouses our ire —from the content of his words.

Many of us have devised various strategies for evading criticism. If you manage to thwart your critic with clever techniques, you may smile to yourself at having turned the tables on him, but afterward he will realize what you've done. You will have acquired an enemy — and lost a valuable resource.

If you are one of those lucky people who still have critics, make sure to hold on to them. If very few dare criticize you, whether because of your high position or because you used to cut critics down, do everything in your power now to encourage these precious few. They are your last hope for self-improvement.

Here are some suggestions for listening to criticism. First, a list of don'ts.

Don't interrupt. While he is talking, make sure not even to use hand gestures or facial expressions that convey disagreement.

Don't change the subject as if you didn't hear what he said. It may have taken a lot of courage for him to approach you; don't take his efforts lightly.

Don't apologize hastily in order to get rid of him. That's a cheap trick for closing the matter quickly.

Don't cast doubt on his right to judge you ("Look who's talking!").

Don't criticize him. Now it's his turn; don't turn the tables and use this particular opportunity to help him through constructive criticism.

Don't impugn his motives for criticizing you. Relate only to his argument. His motives don't diminish the severity of your mistake.

Don't counterattack ("You're overly sensitive"; "It's impossible to satisfy you"; "You always have complaints").

Don't explain what motivated your action. The reasons that caused you to err are less important than what you should do to improve.

Don't blame others for your mistakes. No excuse changes the fact that you made a mistake. Accepting full responsibility allows you to evaluate what went wrong and prevent future recurrences.

Don't show excessive regret ("Oh, no!" Gasp. "How could I have done such a terrible thing!"). If your critic thinks you are a highly sensitive soul, he will be careful not to criticize you again.

Don't laugh it off. That shows disrespect and is very hurtful.

Don't put words in his mouth. Don't exaggerate his complaint in order to rebut it. If he complains that you hurt his feelings, don't say, "You say I'm a liar?" and then prove that you aren't.

Don't intensify his complaint and then feign hurt until *he* winds up apologizing to *you*.

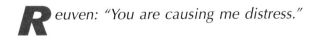

*R*euven: *"You are causing me distress."*

Shimon: "What do you mean I always *cause you distress?* Have you forgotten all the favors I've done for you?"

Note how adroitly Shimon added a word — "always" — that Reuven hadn't said.

Try to recall how you reacted the last few times someone criticized you. How many of the techniques on this list did you use? Resolve right now not to do it again.

On the Positive Side

When someone criticizes you, try to react in a positive way. Encourage him to continue helping you improve. This may require breaking old habits. Remember that every positive step you take will strengthen you and ultimately help you become more effective.

Here are some suggestions for accepting criticism in good spirit, getting the most out of it, and encouraging your critics to come back again with more.

Hear the critic out to the end. Listen with full attention. Look him straight in the eye to show him that you take him seriously. Try to get to the bottom of it and find out precisely what bothers him about your behavior.

Show him that you got the message. Let him know that you've taken his criticism to heart ("Thank you for calling this to my attention; I'll try to do better next time"). If you don't agree, make sure he comes away feeling that you listened carefully and understood him. Sum up his message in your own words and thank him before clarifying your side.

Analyze his words and see what added benefit you can obtain from them. If they lead you to new insights or ideas, share your discoveries with him. Give him the feeling that he has helped you and that you are grateful.

Ask him how you could do better — not to fluster him, but to pinpoint what bothers him ("How do you think I should behave in such a situation? What reaction do you think would be proper?").

Clarify exactly what harm resulted. If you discover that no harm was caused to you, to the critic, or to anyone else, perhaps the criticism was exaggerated.

Accept blame. Admit that you were wrong and convey your sorrow over the incident. Apologize once or twice — but not more; that would make him uncomfortable.

Express sincere sorrow for his pain. Even if it was because he misconstrued something you said or did, the fact is that he felt hurt. So instead of "You shouldn't have taken it that way" — which is a criticism of him — say, "I'm sorry you feel that way. I didn't mean it like that, but next time I'll be more careful to prevent such distressing misinterpretations."

Some critics will react to your apology by enthusiastically rehashing your mistake. You have a right to ask them to stop. These are not the kind you are looking for, so no harm will come of tactfully dropping them from your circle of critics — just be careful not to make enemies of them.

Remember to use this information on the benefit of criticism only when it is directed at you. When it comes to criticizing others, watch out! Not everyone knows what you have just learned.

There's no limit to how far you can go. Use every means at your disposal to get there, including criticism — even if it hurts.

While using every tool to climb higher and higher, bear in mind that you don't have to be perfect.

You Don't Have to Be Perfect

n what colors do you see the world? Optimists are said to see everything in rosy hues, pessimists in shades of gray.

Some see the world in black and white. They are the perfectionists. As far as they're concerned, whatever isn't white as snow is pitch black.

In a perfectionist's eyes, anything less than 100 percent is zero. He evaluates each thing in absolute terms; it is either absolutely good or absolutely evil. And he makes uncompromisingly high demands on himself. He picks on himself constantly, puts down his every good trait, and points to his mistakes as proof of his utter worthlessness.

There is indeed a positive side to this. Perfectionists strive with all their might to do what is good and right in the eyes of G-d and man, and their strong conscience stands vigil 24 hours a day. But they may lose more than they gain. They live in constant tension, fearing that they won't succeed in making the mark. Their stress and lack of joy is dangerous. Many have fallen on the altar of perfection, crushed beneath a yoke too heavy to bear.

Perfectionists lose out in another way as well. They are unlikely to begin working in any area until they are sure beyond all doubt of 100 percent success — a constraint that limits them severely.

The Inevitable Gap

One thing a perfectionist (and everyone else) needs to be aware of is the nature of aspiration. Aspiration is what gives us the push to work and move ahead; if we were satisfied with our present situation, we wouldn't lift a finger to change it. By definition, we aspire to a goal that is some distance beyond where we are now. It follows that there is always a gap between our goal and us, between where we want to get and where we are now, between what we want and what we have.

So it is understandable that we always feel that we have attained less than we want. Whoever has one wants two; that's how G-d made us. No one is ever satisfied with what he has. "No one leaves this world with half of his desires fulfilled" (*Koheles Rabbah* 1:13). There's nothing wrong with that!

It takes wisdom to know how to live in that gap between the ideal and the real. We need to balance our ambition so that it doesn't become so strong that we break or so weak that we rest complacently. And we must learn to accept ourselves as we are, even while we strive to improve.

Many talented people fail because they don't accept themselves; they are looking for perfection. They don't understand that we must work with the talents that the Creator has given us.

The Baal Shem Tov taught that conceit can drive a person out of his mind. He sets himself a goal that is beyond his abilities and becomes insane when he fails to reach it (*Imrei Pinchas* 166).

The Apta Rebbe elaborated.

We have seen many pious Jews become insane or depressed. Where does it come from? From the Torah? Heaven forbid! The Torah gladdens the heart, which is why our Sages forbade Torah study on Tishah B'Av and when one is in mourning (*Taanis* 39a). From mitzvos? "The commandments of Hashem are upright, gladdening the heart" (*Tehillim* 19:9).

Rather, these people want to ascend to G-d without climbing the ladder. They don't serve Him gradually. They grab something that is inappropriate for them without permission from Heaven to do so.

There are also people who serve G-d mainly so that they will be "on a high level." Of this it is written (*Shemos* 20:23), "You shall not ascend My Altar *b'maalos*" — in order to be on a high level — "so that your nakedness will not be exposed on it," as we see that people become depressed. This is not the way of wholesome people; they are satisfied to be G-d's servants and do not seek high levels (*Ohev Yisrael, Vayikra*).

Looking at Yourself and Others

A perfectionist is liable to see himself as a failure if he is not as brilliant as Reuven, as practical as Shimon, as righteous as Levi, as kind as Yehudah, as industrious as Dan, as charming as Naftali, as organized as Gad, as strong as Asher, as considerate as Yissachar, as good looking as Zevulun. Someone quipped about the verse, "One man out of a thousand I have found" (*Koheles* 7:28) — to make one perfect person, you would have to combine the best qualities of a thousand.

If the electricity in our house short-circuits, we are not embarrassed to admit that we don't know how to fix it ourselves; without a second thought, we call an electrician. If a water pipe springs a leak, we are not ashamed to confess our ignorance about plumbing; we don't hesitate to call a plumber. But when we are stuck in an impasse in life, why do we have difficulty admitting that we don't know what to do?

The reason is simple. No one expects us to be electricians or plumbers, and no one is ashamed of his lack of enlightenment in this area. But in other areas of life, they *do* expect us all to be completely capable and all-knowing, to meet with everyone's approval, and to never make a mistake.

But just a minute. Who are "they"? Does anyone really expect us to be perfect — or is it we who demand it of ourselves?

Perfectionists generally focus on those who are more successful than they are, and that is what breaks them. "The fact that he is more successful than me," they tell themselves, "shows that I didn't do enough, and I'm not okay." This is fundamentally wrong and unfair.

It's impossible to do everything perfectly, just as it's impossible to be flawless. All of us are imperfect.

I once heard a giant of Torah say that no matter how far one gets in knowledge of Torah, there is always someone who got further. No matter what we do and how we do it, there will always be someone who can do it better. That's simply how the world is. There will always be someone who earns more money, bakes better bread, or plays violin more skillfully. It doesn't show any weakness or lack on our part, and does not indicate that we have no good points.

Only one person can be "the best." If you think that whoever isn't the best is worthless, you've consigned all of humanity to the garbage dump.

Yes, you should aspire to improve; everyone should. But that's a far cry from thinking that you are worthless because some people do better. Such thoughts only push you further away from perfection.

The Cause

Behind a perfectionist there are often parents who tried to encourage him to be the best and to do everything in the best way possible. Perhaps they wanted their child to succeed where they themselves had failed. So they prodded him to strain himself more and more but were never satisfied with his achievements. They didn't understand that by attacking him for bringing home an 85, they taught him that anything less than 100 is zero.

> *A*lthough Malkah Feld was the youngest girl in her high school, her name was always at the top of the honor roll. When the school ran a contest to encourage the study of Navi, she studied day and night. The results were announced at an assembly, and a great fuss was made over the winners — one of whom, not surprisingly, was Malkah.
>
> Malkah came home with her prize and showed it proudly to her mother.
>
> "How many winners were there?" asked Mrs. Feld.
>
> "Five," said Malkah.
>
> "What number were you?"
>
> "Third."
>
> Mrs. Feld was disappointed. "Why not first?"

Such messages, repeated regularly, teach a child that whatever he does isn't good enough. Since there's no way to satisfy his parent, he may stop trying. Or he may try even harder, not realizing that he is being pushed to climb to the top of a tree of infinite height. Obediently, he learns to demand of

himself the impossible, thereby dooming himself to permanent failure and heartache. He will believe that if only he had
"really" tried, he would have reached the lofty goals that were
set for him. He blames himself for failing and concludes that
something is wrong with him.

As I always say, don't blame your parents. You need to
know that you weren't born this way; you have merely
acquired a bad habit — and habits can be changed.

Exercises

If you have a tendency to search for perfection, you can
and must work on eliminating it. Even if you only manage to
weaken the tendency, you will gain great relief.

As we have seen, the way to change a habit is by doing
opposite actions. To break the deadly habit of perfectionism,
start deliberately doing imperfect actions.

*Nachman suffered most from his perfectionism
when it came to tests. He would go into tremendous stress a few days before any test — and he had
at least one a week — although he couldn't remember
the last time he had gotten less than 100. He couldn't
sleep the night before, and the morning of the test he
would invariably get a stomach ache.*

*"During the next three weeks," I told him, "make
sure not to get more than 80 on any test."*

*"Do you mean to tell me," he asked incredulously,
"that I shouldn't answer correctly even if I know the
answers?"*

*"Exactly," I replied. "Let's see what will happen if
you don't get 100."*

*After that, we went on to various other exercises,
such as each day telling a friend one silly thing he had
done or saying he didn't understand something even
though he did. I asked him to make a list of things he*

"must" do right, and each week he chose two or three items to deliberately do wrong. Eventually he got accustomed to doing things imperfectly and living with it.

The method does wonders. It's also the best way to help people who suffer from obsessive-compulsive disorder, discussed at the end of this chapter.

By deliberately doing things imperfectly, you will get used to acting with serenity and making do with less-than-perfect behavior — which, paradoxically, is the only way to reach your personal perfection.

Torah Lishmah

*"**H**ow can I imbue my son with the desire to learn Torah lishmah?" Mr. Bluth asked me.*

"How old is your son?" I asked.

"Seven," he answered.

"Perhaps you could explain to me," I said, "how you, at the age of 35, acquired this lofty level?"

That threw him. But he was honest enough to reply that he still had a long way to go.

The subject of Torah *lishmah* — studying Torah for the sake of the mitzvah of Torah study alone — confuses many good people, especially teenage yeshivah students just starting off. When they expect to be able to study for the sake of Heaven and to serve G-d without any ulterior motives, they are asking for something that is diametrically opposed to nature, especially at such a young age. They are climbing a tall ladder from which they are liable to fall and sustain a spiritually fatal blow. In fact, I've seen many fine boys who studied Torah diligently, carefully observed every mitzvah, and were interested only in serving G-d — but thought it was worthless since the *lishmah* was missing. They became depressed as a result.

Learning *lishmah* is an extremely lofty level that can be attained only after many years of work. Moreover, whoever tries to learn only *lishmah* is bound to fail! R' Yaakov Yosef of Polonah, a disciple of the Baal Shem Tov, brings various proofs:

> The Gemara teaches that "a person should always study Torah for other motives, because from that he will come to *lishmah*" (Pesachim 50b). "Always" indicates that the only way of ever getting to *lishmah* is by starting off otherwise. If he tries to start off by studying *lishmah*, the evil inclination will prevent him from studying Torah altogether!

❖ ❖ ❖

> King David rose at midnight to study Torah (Berachos 3b). But he knew, said the Baal Shem Tov, that if he intended to wake up for the sake of Heaven, the evil inclination would stop him. So "I considered my ways" — David woke up with the intention of doing things that didn't upset the evil inclination; and afterward, "I returned my feet to Your testimonies" (Tehillim 119:59) — he was able to study Torah without disturbance.

❖ ❖ ❖

> This is the hidden meaning behind the Israelites' request to pass through Edomite territory on their way to the Holy Land (Bamidbar 20:14–18). The Edomite territory is this world — for Esav (Edom) and Yaakov had divided the two worlds between them: Esav chose this world, Yaakov the next. The Jews asked the evil inclination, represented by Edom, for permission to pass through this world serving the King of kings

lishmah: "On the King's road shall we travel. We shall
not veer right or left" — we want to serve Him for the
sake of Heaven, not to gain long life, wealth, or honor,
of which it is written, "Length of days is at [the Torah's]
right; at its left, wealth and honor" (Mishlei 3:16).

To this the evil inclination replied: If you wanted to
begin serving G-d for other motives, I would let you.
But since you want to serve Him *lishmah,* "you shall
not pass through me, lest I go out against you with
the sword!" Under no circumstances will I allow you
to serve G-d in such a manner (Toldos Yaakov Yosef,
Chukas).

The Vilna Gaon teaches the same principle:

*"If your foe is hungry, feed him bread; and if he is thirsty,
give him water to drink" (Mishlei 25:21) — take the evil
inclination along when you go to study Torah, which is
the food of the soul. Don't try to learn lishmah, for then
he will stop you. Begin with more mundane motives; he
will self-destruct, and then you will be able to go on to
lishmah. As the Gemara says: "If this villain attacks you,
draw him to the beis midrash. If he is a stone, he will
melt; if iron, he will be shattered" (Succah 52). The rule
is, "A person should always study Torah for other
motives, because from that he will come to lishmah."*

*The Reishis Chochmah wrote (Gidul Banim 7): If it is
hard for a youngster to constantly be diligent about his
studying, prompt him with things that little children like,
such as honey, roasted grain, nuts, and the like, and tell
him, "This is for you on condition that you go to school
and learn."*

*When he grows more and despises these things, tell
him, "Go to school and learn, and I will buy you a nice
belt and fine shoes."*

When he is older, tell him, "I will give you money so that you will learn."

When he gets bigger, tell him, "Study Torah, and you will be called a proper disciple."

When he understands more, tell him, "Learn, and you will be called Rabbi."

And when he understands more, tell him, "Study Torah and you will be called sage, judge, and head of the court, and you will sit at the head."

Eventually his understanding will attain the truth of Torah, and he will despise all these things and study Torah lishmah, for from other motives he will come to lishmah.

Let's be satisfied with the promise of the *Reishis Chochmah* that even after we study Torah to be called a sage, we still have a chance of reaching the level of *lishmah*. In case you're still not convinced, *Rambam* says the same (*Commentary on the Mishnah, Sanhedrin* 10).

If this is true for everyone, it is especially true for young yeshivah students who have barely begun life! They should study with ardor and enthusiasm, whatever the source of their motivation. In the course of time, after they have spent many years of toiling in the service of G-d, He will surely help them attain this lofty level.

Obsessive-Compulsive Disorder

Even more miserable than those with low self-confidence who are looking for the "right" way or for perfection are those who suffer from obsessive-compulsive disorder (OCD).

OCD sufferers have an uncontrollable inner drive to do certain things with meticulous exactness. This keeps them in a state of stress, and, if they don't succeed, throws them into panic. They often make a ritual out of simple actions, following rigid procedures that they set for themselves: They may put on their clothes only in a certain order, wash their hands innumerable times in the course of the day, bathe once a week for a fixed amount of time, or go to sleep only if their bed has been made in a certain way. These acts appear to start with magical thinking that their action or thought will reduce some risk. OCD sufferers are usually full of doubts; they hesitate to make even small, unimportant decisions.

OCD can show up in a broad variety of irrational behaviors. Howard Hughes, billionaire industrialist and media mogul, stayed locked in his apartment for many years lest he be exposed to germs. Before he would eat, he had his silverware sterilized, after which the handles were wrapped in tissue paper, then tape, and finally tissue paper again. He didn't go for treatment. Shame and hiding the problem are parts of the illness.

OCD is relatively common; it afflicts over 2 percent of the world population. Among religious Jews, it may show up as fear of not fulfilling a mitzvah properly. Reuven makes *hataras nedarim* every day in case he made a vow during a dream and then forgot his dream. Shimon spends 20 minutes each morning checking whether the straps of his head-*tefillin* are on straight.

Many more people suffer from this disturbance than you think, but out of shame, they hide it well from the eyes of onlookers. Some even hide it from their own family members, who don't know how to identify the disturbance.

If your child or student behaves in such a way, don't try to "help" him by pointing out to him that he is "behaving in a foolish way" or "seeking attention." Accusations only double his suffering. OCD sufferers are well aware that their actions are irrational and abnormal. They are ashamed of being driven to do strange things against their will, but are powerless to stop. There is no way to heal this behavior without professional intervention. Sometimes medication is necessary.

Warning: Don't start suspecting that every caprice of a child or teenager is OCD! Leave the diagnosis to a professional.

The Driving Force

hope this book has given you some helpful tools for setting a goal and reaching it. But what happens after you reach your goal?

People are strange creatures. They want to attain something, wear themselves out working hard to get it, and at long last they succeed. Do they heave a sigh of relief, relax, and enjoy their achievement? Surprisingly enough, no. A new aspiration is immediately born within them — twice as big as the first.

> "It is a sorry task that G-d has given to the sons of man with which to be concerned" (Koheles 1:13). No one leaves this world with half of his desires fulfilled. He who has a hundred wants to make it two hundred, and he who has two wants to make it four (Koheles Rabbah).

This calls to mind the adult who dangles a candy just beyond a child's reach. The child drags over a chair and clambers up in the hope of getting the candy — whereupon the adult picks his hand up higher.

What good does it do us to have ambition rampant in our hearts? The Creator certainly did not put this nature into man for nothing. Why did He make us like this?

To Be Completed

When G-d created the world, He did not bring it to perfection. Intentionally, He left room for man to complete it. The Torah says that on the seventh day, "G-d abstained from all His work, which G-d created *to make*" (*Bereishis* 2:3) — to be brought to completion (*Rashi, Bamidbar Rabbah* 42:3).

> *A philosopher asked R' Hoshaya, "If circumcision is precious [to G-d], why didn't He create Adam circumcised?"*
>
> *R' Hoshaya explained, "Everything created in the six days of creation needs more done to it. Mustard must be sweetened and wheat must be ground. Even man needs to be completed" (Bereishis Rabbah 11:7).*

Man himself is the crown of Creation, yet G-d didn't create him perfectly ready to carry out his mission on earth. G-d indeed planted in each person the traits and talents that he will need to fulfill his special mission — but only in potential. It's up to us to actualize this potential, developing our traits and talents in a positive way so that they become useful tools for carrying out our mission.

Thus we are born with a lack — and we have a tremendous will and desire to fill it. A normal child starts out in life with irrepressible energy and unflagging spirit to conquer the world. He's constantly on the go. Adults get tired just from watching him. Although this energy is often derailed and dampened by society, parents, teachers, and life events, a secret force inside continues driving him to fill his every lack. Never is he content with what he has. He strives relentlessly to attain possessions, improve his status, gather power and influence, take control and change things. At the root of all his actions is a single motive: to attain what he still lacks.

Getting on Track

To serve G-d takes effort, and to make the effort takes a strong will and great yearning. From where will a person get these? From the desire that he naturally has for physical and material things!

We speak of *yetzer hatov,* "the good inclination," and *yetzer hara,* "the evil inclination." But R' Tzaddok HaKohen of Lublin explains that the root of the *yetzer* is not evil! *Yetzer* simply means a powerful drive and will, which a person can use for either good or bad (*Takanas HaShavin* 32b). The essence of a person is this *yetzer;* it is what makes him greater than the angels. "Whoever is greater than his friend, his *yetzer* is greater" (*Succah* 52a) — his greatness stems from the greater will and desire burning in his heart! (*Tzidkas HaTzaddik* 248).

The Patriarchs were called *eisanim* (*Rosh Hashanah* 11a), which means "stubborn" — they had a consuming desire that burned relentlessly until it was satisfied. This powerful *yetzer* drove Avraham to the pinnacle of love for G-d; Yitzchak, to the pinnacle of fear of G-d; and Yaakov, to the pinnacle of love with fear (*Tzidkas HaTzaddik* 248).

If you have a great desire for physical pleasures, don't think it's a defect in you. On the contrary, it makes you all the more suitable for loving G-d and searching passionately for truth (*Tzidkas HaTzaddik* 44). Don't try to break your nature; don't extinguish the fiery passion that burns inside you. It can get you very far, if only you guide it in positive directions. Use it for serving G-d! Transfer your physical desires and aspirations to spiritual tracks.

G-d does not ask you to break your natural characteristics, or *middos,* but to elevate them. The Chozeh of Lublin said, "If a person breaks a *middah,* he gets two." The only thing to do with a *middah* is to use it for good.

Take pride, for instance. The praise of Judah's righteous King Yehoshaphat is that "his heart was proud in the ways of Hashem" (*II Divrei HaYamim* 17:6). Although arrogance is akin to idolatry, we are not asked to destroy our pride, but to channel it into the service of G-d.

R' Yosef Yozel of Novardok taught that no trait is intrinsically "good" or "bad"; it all depends on how you use it. The word *middah* itself means "measure"; you have to know when and how much to use each *middah* (*Madregas HaAdam*).

The Gemara relates that the Men of the Great Assembly wanted to utterly destroy the evil inclination. But after they had restrained it for three days, they sought a day-old egg (בִּיעֲתָא) all over the Land of Israel and could not find one. Upon seeing that the world could not endure without the evil inclination, they decided not to destroy it (*Yoma* 69b).

The Maggid of Mezeritch interprets בִּיעֲתָא as "prayer" (like the similar word בְּעָיוּ in *Yeshayahu* 21:12). They couldn't find a prayer. Why? Because prayers require fervor; special prayers require extra fervor. A cold person may pray with fear and awe, but fervor requires a passionate temperament — the fire of the evil inclination. They wanted to pray for someone who had gotten sick that day, but since there was no evil inclination in the world, fervor was lacking! (the Chozeh of Lublin, *Zos Zikaron*).

Not only doesn't passion disturb our service of G-d; it helps us ascend to higher and higher levels of Torah study and mitzvah observance.

Good and Very Good

We can now understand why G-d gave us a generous helping of desire that drives us forward relentlessly. He deliberately refrained from completing creation, including man. He wants us to do it. And to do it, we need will and insatiable desire.

This is the power that drives the world forward. This is what produces change in the individual and in society. People always aspire to advance, whether in spiritual or in material matters. They work day and night to invent things that raise the standard of living. Were people satisfied with what they had, we would still be living in caves and riding donkeys. The world of Torah has certainly been developed by men of vision and energy, who are never satisfied with the present situation and who aspire with all their might to expand the turf of holiness and increase the glory of Torah.

Thus the evil inclination is *very* good. "G-d saw all that He had made, and behold it was very good" (*Bereishis* 1:31). What is meant by "very good"? "Good" refers to the good inclination, says the Midrash, "very" — to the evil inclination. Is the evil inclination very good? Yes, indeed. Without it, man would not build a house, marry, beget children, or work (*Koheles Rabbah* 3:16).

The *yetzer* is what makes a person. This mighty force can push him to the pinnacles of service of G-d. Great blessing is hidden in the drive to advance, acquire, and conquer. This is one of the secrets of creation.

That's not all. G-d created man with a feeling of lack that pushes him to always aspire to more because accomplishing is what makes life interesting and exciting, and what brings him true joy and pleasure.

The Baal Shem Tov went so far as to say that G-d created man to have ups and down in his service of G-d, "because permanent pleasure becomes nature and is no longer pleasure. These ups and down allow him to have real pleasure, which is fundamental in serving G-d" (*Toldos Yaakov Yosef, Tazria, Shelach*).

Enjoy and succeed!

Epilogue

I don't believe in trying to calm dissatisfied people by convincing them that everything is okay. It doesn't work and it isn't right. If a person who isn't satisfied with himself comes to me, I try to help him accept what he can't change — but I try to *increase* his dissatisfaction with things that he *can* change.

If you are sitting at a table with a royal feast spread before you, and you are given permission to take as much as you want, isn't it laughable to take only a crumb of bread and then complain bitterly that you've been left hungry? If you aren't satisfied with this portion, reach out and take another piece — and another, and another — until you satisfy your hunger.

This applies to all realms of life, including the spiritual. G-d gave each of us the freedom to choose good or bad. The choice is yours. No one can prevent you from acting in matters that affect you, and no one can overcome for you the obstacles you face.

If you don't reach out to increase your share of life, don't blame anyone else. No one is guilty of the fact that you remained "hungry." A person who doesn't study should not complain about the meagerness of his knowledge, and a person who sits back with his hands folded should not complain that he has no satisfaction in life.

If you want more out of life, extend your hand and take another slice!

You have the ability. Shake off your fears! Sharpen your mind, improve your skills, and work hard in areas that interest you! You will succeed spectacularly and will be filled with satisfaction and happiness.

If the owner of a big department store were to allow people to enter for two hours and take anything they could free of charge, what would you think of someone who took only water or chatted with a friend instead of selecting expensive merchandise?

G-d created a big world, and He allows us to choose whatever we want, but He warned us to choose the good and shun the evil. Isn't it foolish to waste the opportunity?

Our life is before us! Instead of wasting precious time complaining, worrying, and making excuses about what can't be changed, let's improve what we can and make the most of what we have. What are we waiting for?

A wise man once said: The world is divided into three: people who make things happen, people who watch others make things happen, and people who always ask, "What happened?"

No one willingly joins the third group, but what about the first two? Do we want to stand like sticks of wood and watch others succeed, or do we want to be winners?

If we invest in ourselves, if we make sure to add to our knowledge and wisdom all the time, if we invest continual efforts in improving our character traits and our personal abilities, surely G-d will help us to be among the doers. We'll accomplish great things for the public welfare as well as for our own.

Wake up! The choice is in your hands! Don't make peace with what you are!

Don't begin with the assumption that you can't do much! The sky's the limit! Change your approach! Make sure that each day you acquire more mitzvos and good deeds than yesterday, that each day you are wiser than you were yesterday, that each day you take action to bring yourself closer to your goal.

Go out and succeed. May G-d be with you!